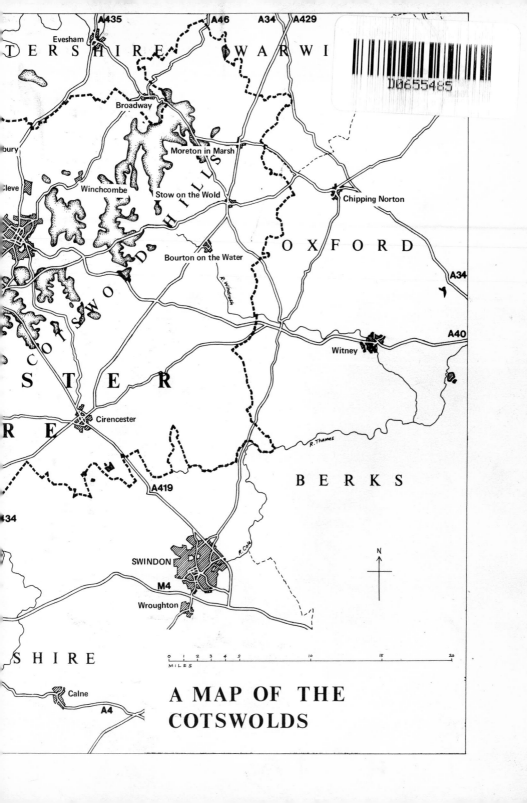

A MAP OF THE COTSWOLDS

HISTORY, PEOPLE, AND PLACES

in

THE COTSWOLDS

The Swan Inn at Minster Lovell

History, People, and Places
in
THE COTSWOLDS

J. ALLAN CASH

SPURBOOKS LIMITED

Published by
SPUR BOOKS LTD.
1 Station Road,
Bourne End,
Buckinghamshire.

© J. ALLAN CASH   1974

S B N   0 902875 59 0

Printed in Great Britain by Compton Printing Ltd.
London and Aylesbury.

Contents

Page No.

LIST OF ILLUSTRATIONS   6

BIBLIOGRAPHY   9

INTRODUCTION   11

CHAPTER I   People Through the Ages   14

CHAPTER II   Following the Windrush   18

CHAPTER III   Following the Escarpment—to Cheltenham   46

CHAPTER IV   The Escarpment—Cheltenham to Painswick   74

CHAPTER V   The Southern Cotswolds   84

CHAPTER VI   Following the River Coln   112

CHAPTER VII   The River Churn   132

CHAPTER VIII   Roman Roads in the Cotswolds   144

CHAPTER IX   Following the Evenlode   153

INDEX   158

ILLUSTRATIONS

		Page
	The Swan Inn at Minster Lovell	Frontispiece
1.	Beech screen near Naunton	11
2.	The interior of Temple Guiting Church	19
3.	The countryside near Naunton, on the River Windrush	20
4.	The pulpit in Naunton Church	21
5.	The Pigeon Cote at Naunton	22
6.	Bourton on the Water and the River Windrush	24
7.	The Model Village, Bourton on the Water	25
8.	The village of Lower Slaughter	27
9.	The Church at Upper Slaughter	28
10.	Upper Slaughter Manor House	29
11.	Clapton Church	30
12.	Great Barrington Church	32
13.	A corner of Taynton Quarries	33
14.	Sherborne House	36
15.	Norman doorway, Burford Church	37
16.	A barrel tomb in Burford churchyard	38
17.	The Bay Tree Hotel, Burford	40
18.	Effigies in Swinbrook Church	42
19.	Minster Lovell ruins and church	43
20.	Pigeon cote at Minster Lovell	44
21.	The Gloucestershire Plain and the Malverns from the Escarpment	47
22.	Chipping Campden Market Hall	48
23.	The Gainsborough Chapel in Chipping Campden Church	49
24.	Almshouses at Chipping Campden	51
25.	The font at Saintbury Church	54
26.	Meeting of the Hunt at the Lygon Arms Hotel, Broadway	56
27.	Broadway Beacon, on Broadway Hill	57
28.	Snowshill Manor	59
29.	The bell-ringer at Snowshill Manor	60
30.	Stanway House, Stanway	62
31.	The village of Stanton	63
32.	Hailes Abbey ruins near Winchcombe	65
33.	On Cleeve Hill above Cheltenham	66
34.	A gargoyle on Winchcombe Church	68
35.	Belas Knap Burial Mound	70
36.	The Imperial Gardens, Cheltenham	72

37. Seven Springs, the source of the Thames 75
38. Gloucestershire Plain from Birdlip Hill 76
39. The cloisters of Prinknash Abbey 77
40. Yews at Painswick Church 81
41. The main street of Painswick 82
42. The Severn Valley from Stanley Wood, near Painswick 83
43. The Gloucestershire Plain from Haresfield Hill 85
44. An old lock on the Stroudwater Canal 87
45. The Golden Valley near Stroud 88
46. Chalford, in the Golden Valley, near Stroud 90
47. 13th century effigy, Bisley Church 91
48. The Severn Springs at Bisley 92
49. A Saxon carving in Daglingworth Church 94
50. The Pigeon Cote at Daglingworth 95
51. The Market Hall, Minchinhampton 97
52. The Long Stone, Minchinhampton 98
53. The Mill Pond, Longford's Mill, Nailsworth 99
54. Ozleworth Church 102
55. Wotton under Edge Church 104
56. Downham Hill, near Uley 105
57. Box tombs in Uley churchyard 106
58. Owlpen Manor, near Uley 107
59. Uley from Uley Bury Fort 108
60. Entrance to Hetty Pegler's Tump, Uley 109
61. Brockhampton Manor 113
62. The Pigeon Cote at Withington 114
63. Chedworth Roman Villa, mosaic pavement 115
64. Chedworth Roman Villa – the heating system 116
65. Coln St. Dennis Church 118
66. The River Coln at Coln Rogers 119
67. Bibury Manor 120
68. Arlington Row, Bibury 121
69. Cotswold cottages at Arlington Row, Bibury, Gloucestershire 122
70. The Swan Hotel, Bibury 123
71. A house by the Coln at Quenington 127
72. The Market Square, Fairford 128
73. A stained glass window in Fairford Church 129
74. The Berkeley Tomb in Coberley Church 132
75. Norman font in Rendcomb Church 135
76. North Cerney on the River Churn 137
77. Brasses in Cirencester Church 140

78. Cirencester town and park   142
79. Moreton in Marsh   146
80. A corner of the Market Square at Stow on the Wold   147
81. Northleach Church and village   149

Bibliography

There must have been scores of books written about the Cotswolds, certainly in the last hundred years or so. It is a district I have known since childhood, though I have never lived there. To write a book about the Cotswolds has been a labour of great joy to me, not only bringing back many happy memories but forcing me, in a way, to learn a great deal more about them. Not only have I made several different trips to the Cotswolds during the writing of this book, seeing some new places, revisiting many I knew already, delving into much more detail than I had previously done, but I have looked up information in many different books. I have also written to various people for particular details and have invariably received the greatest help from them. There must be something about the Cotswolds that makes people want to be friendly and helpful, or so it seems to me. David Verey's book on the Cotswolds, in the "Buildings of England" series, has perhaps been the most useful of all, and I have had some pleasant correspondence with him. So my list of books referred to in the course of writing my own book shall start with his;

Gloucestershire: The Cotswolds. By David Verey.
Gloucestershire. By Arthur Mee. The King's England Series.
Oxfordshire. By Arthur Mee. The King's England Series.
The Cotswolds. Ward Locke Red Guide.
Portraits of Rivers. Edited by Eileen Molony.
Gloucestershire. By Kenneth Hare. (Robt. Hale County Book).
Shell Guides to Gloucestershire.
Roman Britain. By I. A. Richmond. (Pelican).
The Changing Face of England. By Anthony Collett.
A Book of Dovecotes. By A. O. Cooks.
The Cotswolds and the Upper Thames. By James Dyer.
The Cotswold Year. By Warren.
English Social History. By G. M. Trevelyan.
Wold Without End. By H. J. Massingham.
Gloucestershire and the Cotswolds. Spurbooks.
Numerous booklets and leaflets of places, churches and other buildings, an invaluable source of information.

THE COTSWOLDS

The Cotswolds, as the name indicates, is a district of rolling hills and valleys, a large area of some 1,000 square miles, stretching from well into Oxfordshire nearly to the Severn River, but mostly in Gloucestershire. Its boundaries are not clearly defined, nor need they be, for the stone-built villages of western Oxfordshire, even of parts of Berkshire and Wiltshire, are much the same as those which make the Cotswolds so famous. The towns and villages are built from the local mellow oolitic limestone which ages so naturally and softens itself with lichen and moss, and so rounds off the newness and sharp edges.

Some of the very best of the Cotswold villages occur below the hills, on the edge of the Severn Plain, and they cannot be left out simply because they do not stand some hundreds of feet above the surrounding countryside. So our Cotswold boundaries must be quite flexible.

Much of the Cotswold region consists of an undulating table-land, with winding streams cutting deep into the land. The table-land rises gradually towards the west and ends in a steep escarpment running for many miles, dominating the Severn Plain and Valley far below. Thus various distinct types of country emerge in the Cotswolds.

There are broad, often level uplands, windswept and exposed, with not many trees but sometimes windscreens of beeches, long narrow woods beside the road. Fields and stone walls and isolated farms

Beech screen near Naunton

dominate the uplands, with good crops and many sheep. And sheep have done much to mould the history of this land.

There are deep green valleys, with placid trout streams and sheltered little villages every few miles. Virtually all the buildings are made of the mellow Cotswold stone, often looking as though they had always been there, as natural a part of the scene as the trees and bushes and the rivers themselves. Every village has a church, some famous, some pre-Norman, all fitting perfectly into the landscape. Cotswold villages are among the most beautiful in all Britain, and there are so many of them.

The escarpment is quite remarkable, with its vast views across the Severn Basin and the Gloucester Plain. Naturally, there are some special outlook points, such as Broadway Hill with its Beacon. The steep edge tapers off north of Chipping Campden and on to Hidcote in the north. Meon Hill stands out as a last bastion, with an ancient British fort on top. Villages lie below, such as Aston-sub-Edge, Weston-sub-Edge, and nearby is Willersey and Broadway, Buckland, Stanton and Stanway, some of the gems of all the Cotswold villages. Broadway is rather too well known now and too popular but the others are little visited by crowds of any kind.

There are other look-out points—Cleeve Hill, above Cheltenham, and close by, Nottingham Hill above Bishop's Cleeve, less well known. There is Leckhampton Hill, south of Cheltenham, with splendid walks and even cliffs. And a whole host of hill tops above Brockworth—Crickley Hill, South Hill, Shab Hill. Then Birdlip, a tiny village at the top of a prodigious hill of 1 in 5 and part of a Roman road, with Cooper's Hill and many a viewpoint from the woods overhanging the Severn Plain all along towards Stroud on A-46.

On many of the hills there are ancient forts and earth-works and tumuli, for this was a well populated area of Britain long before Romans, Saxons, Danes and Normans came to modernise and change forever the land that was ancient Britain, with its great forests and wild animals and perhaps not such primitive tribes.

Outcrops of the escarpment, standing out like islands in the plain, are often famous landmarks. Bredon Hill is one, ringed by a clutch of pretty villages—Elmley Castle, though little of the castle is left now, Ashton-under-Hill, Overbury, Grafton, Conderton, Bredons Norton, and Great Comberton. Dumbleton Hill is another, with Dumbleton and its hall and estate below, and Oxenton Hill above Teddington, all standing out like worn-down craters of volcanoes.

So the Cotswolds consist of the high, open table-lands, the lush green valleys cut deep into them, the rugged escarpment with its vast ranging woods and steep hills, and the villages scattered below the slopes in the lowlands, on the edge of the rich farmlands.

We could do worse than follow the main rivers from their sources in the Cotswold hills to where they leave the district. They mostly flow into the Thames eventually, for as we have seen, the Cotswold Plateau slopes down gradually east and southwards from the high edge of the escarpment and so the rivers run down from it to join the larger river.

From the east, the first of these rivers is the Evenlode, then the Windrush, a few miles further west, followed by the Coln, and finally the Churn, which is the name of the river that rises at Seven Springs and becomes the Thames itself. All are more or less parallel, each has its special charm and leads the explorer past strings of exquisite Cotswold villages and through some of the loveliest scenery in England. Westwards from the Churn the rivers are smaller. They rise in the high southern hills for the most part but break out through gaps in the escarpment and run into the Severn. We will have a look at them all in turn.

We will certainly follow the Thames, for both its long-disputed sources rise in the Cotswolds and join near Cricklade to become the noblest river in England. And we will run the whole length of the great escarpment, as close along the edge as we can, all the way from Hidcote and Meon Hill to Stroud and Wotton-under-Edge. And as this was such a well-settled Roman area, we will follow the Roman roads—Akeman Street, Fosse Way, Ermine Street and others as they stride relentlessly in dead straight lines across the Cotswold Hills and valleys. It is a noble and beautiful part of Britain and one of the most historical, ranging from the earliest times right up to the present day.

But before we start our explorations, let us see who the people were, from the earliest times, who lived in the Cotswolds and in various ways left their mark upon them.

13

CHAPTER I

People Through the Ages

There are signs of human habitation in Britain going back as much as five hundred thousand years ago—man-made tools among the bones of mammoths, etc.—long before England was separated from the Continent. Even 25,000 years ago, the Early Stone Age people lived in some sort of settlements. But it was the Late Stone Age men, who arrived about 2,500 B.C., who really began to make a profound change in the ways of life in this country. These were the people who built Stonehenge and Avebury. But more important still, they had learnt to cultivate cereals and to domesticate animals. Thus they began to settle in permanent villages and towns, and to build forts to protect themselves, as well as quite elaborate long burial tombs. Remains of these various works are clearly visible in the Cotswolds today, though there is nothing in the way of a Stonehenge in size.

Domestic dwellings, as in most parts of the world, were not made of such enduring materials and so there are few remains of them anywhere. But the pottery made by these early settlers and the flint instruments they made—axe heads, knives, picks and arrow-heads—tell us much about their way of life. So important was flint that it was carried all over the country from main deposits in the chalk downs, East Anglia, where it was mined, from Scotland, Wales and Ireland. Roughly shaped on the site to save weight, the flints would be carried to areas where they were in demand, to be finished there by the local people. This took place during the late Neolithic period well into the Bronze Age.

Then, when methods of making and working bronze were developed, flints were no longer required. Later still, from about 550 B.C. to the coming of the Romans in 43 A.D., iron was the common metal, this indeed being the period known as the Iron Age. The long burial tombs of the Cotswolds were built in the late Neolithic Age, from 2,500 B.C. onwards. Most of the hill-top forts in the Cotswolds are from the Iron

Age. Dozens of long barrows have been discovered; there are probably at least a score of hill-top forts in the Cotswolds.

The first Bronze Age men were Celts, from the Iberian Peninsula, round-headed men known as Goidels. They apparently had little success in invading the Cotswold hills, but the next wave of Celts, known as Brythons (Britons) soon covered the whole of this area. They were the people who met the Romans at the time of the invasion in 43 A.D. The Romans were surprised to find quite a civilized people in Britain, men who had armour, chain mail coats and two-wheeled fighting chariots, people who worked gold, bronze, iron and mined tin, exporting it to the Continent. Their religion was Druidism.

The Romans marched inland and met the "Budini" or Dobuni people of the Cotswolds, as they were called, eventually defeating them. A Roman camp was built at Corinium, now Cirencester, and a line drawn across the south of Britain to Camulodunum (Colchester) to consolidate their gains. Later, another fortress was built at Glevum (Gloucester) and the River Severn was made a natural barrier between the Romans and the fierce Silures of Wales. The Silures were probably late Stone Age men driven from the Cotswolds by the Celts. They attacked the Romans continuously, so that the Romans built a long chain of forts on almost every hill top along the Cotswold escarpment. Caradoc was King of the Silures—Caractacus to the Romans. After a great pitched battle he was captured, put in chains and sent to Rome, where it is said he created a very good impression.

The Romans soon began to build their famous roads all over conquered Britain. Fosse Way became their main artery through the Cotswolds, with Cirencester as its focal point. The Romans felt safe behind the Severn, but safer still behind the Fosse Way. However, this was only for a time. They later marched northwards, eventually conquering all England, as we know it today. Then Glevum ceased to be so important and declined as a town and fortress. But Corinium gained in importance as a communications and administrative centre and became second only to London.

Villas of wealthy Romans were scattered all over the Cotswolds. Many Romans married the native British women and settled down as farmers and big land owners. The Romans were not barbarians, sacking and pillaging wherever they went, like so many invading hordes throughout history. They were colonizers and civilised people who brought order and progress to all the countries they conquered. They won the hearts of the people with their justice and fairness, gained their co-operation and then merged their talents to run the country together. As the British were far from savages when the Romans came, the two civilizations merged well and Britain became highly prosperous and stable for several hundred years. When the Romans left it was another story altogether.

Early in the 5th Century, the Goths and the Huns invaded Roman Europe and even sacked Rome in 410 A.D. Then the Vandals swept over the Continent, taking Rome in 455 A.D. The Roman Empire was crumbling, the victim of vast outside forces spreading from further east. In that same year, Emperor Honorius absolved Britain from any further allegiance to Rome. This was a disaster for Britain, and especially for the Cotswolds, where a thriving export of wool had been developed. Suddenly the foreign markets disappeared.

Irish pirates began to invade, coming up the Severn. Picts came down into England from the north, while Angles, Saxons and Jutes invaded from the south and east coming from the Lowlands, Denmark and Germany. By 550 A.D. they had reached Fairford. In 577 A.D., a great battle was fought and the people of Glevum, Corinium and Aquae Sulis (Bath) were massacred. Corinium became flooded when the highly intricate water system was neglected and destroyed.

But in spite of all this the Anglo-Saxons, a pretty blood-thirsty lot altogether, though some of them were undoubtedly invited to come to Britain as mercenaries, were not barbarians. Christianity, introduced by St. Augustine in 596 A.D., had a great civilising influence, bringing both literacy and eventually good government, though the whole country was divided for a long time into different kingdoms, such as Mercia, Northumbria and Wessex, warring between each other.

Then, when the country was pretty settled, came the invasions of the Vikings, raids really, for pillage and slaughter, followed in later years by full scale invasion and occupation. King Alfred's defeat of the Vikings in 878 had the effect of bringing them to heel, under Alfred as King at first, and then his successors. Other Norse and Viking invasions occurred later, and in 1016 we find Canute as King of England and of an empire which stretched all the way from the Baltic Sea across England. But weaker monarchs succeeded Canute, so that by the time the Norman invasion came, the country was far from united and fell an easy victim to the new invaders.

The Normans were by no means colonizers like the Romans but very much inclined to barbarism, looting and murder. They were, at the time, a calamity for Britain. But when the fighting stopped, they

16

introduced much of their civilised form of life and their wonderful architecture, and they brought learning and high forms of civilisation to their newly conquered lands. But one thing they failed utterly to do was to make the British learn the French language, despite the formation of special schools for this purpose.

CHAPTER II

Following the Windrush

The River Windrush rises in the sloping fields just north of Cutsdean, close to the edge of the escarpment and only two miles east of Stanway, which is far down below the edge. Almost immediately we find it running in a deep little valley much covered in trees, past Cutsdean itself, though the village stands high above the stream on a hill, to Ford, barely a mile below.

Another mile south, our tiny river reaches Temple Guiting, almost hidden amidst the trees, so near to the main road (B-4077) and yet hardly known to the fast-travelling public. In the 12th Century, Gilbert de Lacey gave these and other properties to the Knights Templars, and thus originated the name Temple Guiting. It is the site of a large pigeon house, part of the particularly fine Tudor Manor Farm nearby. Here also begin signs of the many water mills which were such a feature of all the Cotswold streams.

The Church of St. Mary at Temple Guiting has been almost disguised by many "improvements" throughout the centuries. The chancel is still clearly 12th Century Norman, and bits of the Norman doorway are to be seen in the north porch. The first big changes took place in the 15th Century, and from then on nearly all the original Norman work disappeared and was replaced with whatever the contemporary architecture dictated.

Immediately downstream comes Kineton, a tiny hamlet where fords instead of bridges are used to cross the river. One ancient clapper bridge spans the stream at the lower end, doubtless many centuries old. Then comes Barton, built up on steep banks above the water.

Just below Barton a little tributary comes in from the west, close to Guiting Power, a village with a green surrounded by a jumble of lovely little cottages, truly Cotswold, all corners, gables, roofs and chimneys, delightfully unplanned, some now partly restored. Even the 1918 War Memorial is based on a mediaeval design. And here is a Norman

The interior of Temple Guiting Church

19

church, St. Michael's for once not ruined by restoration. Though added to and enlarged at various times and in various styles, from the 12th Century onwards, it always seems to have been done with great care, even into this century, a remarkable span of good taste and affection. If you look carefully, you will see a Norman priest's door and a small window near it in the chancel, with a plaque stating: "At the restoration of 1903 these were not disturbed," How truly remarkable! There are fine Norman doorways, particularly the one on the south side.

The village contains a 16th Century Manor House, an old bakery of about the same period, and a 17th Century Mill known as the Dyers, on a site mentioned in the Domesday Book, with the wheel still there. Across the river is Guiting Grange, much rebuilt around 1848, in a fine deer park.

Now the Windrush is becoming a sizeable stream and it turns eastward to Naunton, long and straggling on the north bank. The best view of this quite sizeable village is from the main Stow-on-the-Wold

The countryside near Naunton, on the River Windrush

The pulpit in Naunton Church

21

to Cheltenham road riding high up on the hills to the south. It is a typical Cotswold view, down into a deep valley with a square towered church and a village around it, with wide sweeping hills and chequer-board fields beyond. A road runs down to each end of the village from A-436. But we have doubtless reached the village by the valley road which has diverged somewhat to the north.

St. Andrew's Church is a mixture, as usual, but Saxon and Norman details can be found with the later alterations and additions. Its main feature today is the pulpit, of white stone, richly carved and dating from the end of the 14th Century, approximately. A curiosity is a memorial to Dr. William Oldys, "barbarously murthered by ye Rebells in ye yeare 1645", for his loyalty to his King and zeal for the established Church. There is also a tablet to his son, Ambrose, who it is stated, died with better fortune, for he escaped the dangers of battles fought in the service of the King.

Naunton is the site of one of the enormous pigeon cotes that were such a feature of earlier times. This one was built in the 15th Century and is a handsome building with high gables, still in good repair today. It stands a little way from the Manor House with its farm buildings, just above the Windrush, spanned here by a low bridge, a most attractive site.

The Pigeon Cote at Naunton

Perhaps this is the point where we should explain the origin and importance of large pigeon houses. Pigeons were kept essentially as a source of fresh meat during the winter season, the young birds being killed and eaten when they had reached a good size. Cattle and sheep could not be kept in good condition during the long winter months on hay alone, even if there was enough of it. Hence, in the autumn, most of these animals on each farm were killed off and salted down; only a few breeding animals were kept for the future. Salted meat tended to become monotonous when there was no alternative, but young pigeons—squabs—made a most welcome change. Hence the keeping of pigeons in large numbers became very popular. It is estimated that there were no less than 26,000 pigeon cotes in England in the mid-17th Century, averaging five hundred birds each.

The Romans were credited with inventing the pigeon cote and keeping the birds for meat. They called their cotes by the curious name of columbarium. The Normans are believed to be the first people to build them in England. In France they were known as colombiers. They served a double purpose, providing a most valuable manure as well as the meat. In all cases, the pigeons flew freely, eating off the land and devouring nearby crops in a devastating way. Small farmers were extremely angry but, as the pigeon cotes were a privilege of the wealthy land-owner, there was nothing they could do about it. But it is said that this was one cause of the French Revolution, and it might well be. In England it was usually the lords of the manor who were allowed to operate pigeon cotes. Their crops suffered too, of course, but they could better afford the loss, and at least they had the fresh meat.

It was the introduction of turnips and swedes which brought an end to the necessity for pigeon cotes, early in the 18th Century. These provided excellent food for farm animals all through the period when there was not enough grass, and so fresh beef and mutton was available throughout the year. The great pigeon cotes fell into disuse and only a few of them have survived. The one at Naunton had more than a thousand nesting places, all on the inside walls of the building, as was the custom. Often the walls sloped inwards, especially in circular cotes, so that the birds' dropping fell down and could easily be retrieved from the floor.

The once important mill at Naunton, at the east end, is now converted into a private house, its old wooden machinery having been removed only in recent years. The main Stow road crosses the Windrush a mile below Naunton, on Harford Bridge, close by Lower

23

Harford Farm. The present farm was built on a site which preceded Naunton village by possibly centuries, close by a ford which still exists.

Now, with a few big bends, the Windrush passes under Fosse Way, the Roman road, close to Bourton-on-the-Water. This is really a small town but a very beautiful one, notable for its low stone bridges across the river. Most are merely foot bridges, only two will carry cars. But by far the best way to explore Bourton is on foot, and then it is sheer delight, finding odd corners, lovely gardens and a host of delightful Cotswold houses.

Along both banks of the river, especially on the north side, are wide verges of grass, alas now rather too popular with visitors in summer time. But nothing seems to disturb the peace and quiet of this rambling old town for long—can it really be called a town with fewer than three thousand inhabitants? It is off the busy main road and so does not suffer much from through traffic, yet parking space is often hard to find in the summer time.

Bourton church (St. Lawrence), originally Norman on a Saxon site, was largely rebuilt in 1784, though the chancel dates from 1328. The chancel roof is now richly painted and is one of the best features of the church, though it was done only in 1928, by F. E. Howard. He was also

Bourton on the Water and the River Windrush

responsible for the particularly fine carved and painted reredos and other work, making this a truly beautiful church by any standards. The tower, built in 1774, is peculiar in having a leaded dome on the top, most un-Cotswold indeed. With all its changes and additions, it is today an outstanding church in many ways, essentially 19th Century, largely the work of Sir Thomas Jackson, a famous explorer in his day.

There was a Roman settlement close to Bourton, though not a large one, doubtless to guard the Roman bridge across the Windrush, carrying Fosse Way as the modern bridge does today. By the 8th Century this old bridge had gone, superceded by a ford until another stone bridge was built in the 15th Century. Today's bridge dates from 1959.

One of the most popular features of Bourton-on-the-Water is a model of the village on a one-tenth scale, situated behind the Old New Inn. It is a remarkably accurate copy, even including a model of the model village itself, all to scale.

The Model Village, Bourton on the Water

Another attraction in Bourton is Birdland, an outdoor aviary as it were, with penguins, pelicans, flamingoes and gaudy parrots. The parrots and macaws live in houses in the trees all through the Spring and Summer and are often seen flying about the village, though they return in good time for their evening meal and bed time. All this is the creation of Len Hill, who lived as a boy with his parents in the stable yard of a beautiful 16th Century Manor House known as "Chardwar." He was always interested in birds and kept a number as pets.

He became a master builder, modernising and restoring many Cotswold buildings, but never lost his interest in birds. In 1956 he achieved his great ambition by acquiring "Chardwar", with its three and a half acres of gardens. But the garden was a wilderness, and much needed doing in the house. He restored both house and garden and began to collect birds from all over the world. His basic idea was conservation, especially of species likely to disappear. But soon he realised that the public would be interested and he formed Birdland and opened his doors to anyone who was interested.

The place has grown rapidly, with now a fine big tropical house, reproducing the hot humid climate of the tropics, with exotic plants and flowers, even insects, where many birds of wide variety fly about and nest in spacious and natural surroundings. Outside there are pools for penguins, and the graceful pink-hued flamingoes stroll about among the visitors on the lawns. Peter Scott has not only given his blessing to this enterprise but is most enthusiastic about it. Now there is a fine lecture room, with a large mural by Peter Scott. A film of Birdland has been produced and shown all over the world. Birdland is a beautiful and most interesting place; there is nothing like it anywhere else in this country.

Just to the east of the town stands the old Iron Age Fort of Salmonsbury, this time on low-lying ground. It had two banks and ditches and would have had the usual wooden ramparts on the top of the higher bank. It covered perhaps as much as sixty acres altogether. Remains of circular huts have been discovered, as well as pottery, coins and tools. The fort was probably in its prime about five hundred years before Christ.

A couple of miles or so below Bourton, a tributary called the Dikler comes in from the north, flowing down from the Swells, Upper and Lower, two lovely little villages, unfortunately both on busy roads. But a tributary of the Dikler, the River Eye, flows through Upper and Lower Slaughter, the latter now rather too well known, but both almost literally buried in the lush green countryside. Despite the name,

The village of Lower Slaughter

27

nothing could be more beautiful and peaceful than these two little gems of the Cotswolds. Slaughter might well have been derived from a sloe tree which, in days far back, may have been a prominent object in the village, before it even had a name.

The Eye flows through Lower Slaughter, between stone banks, with several foot-bridges across the stream. The truly Cotswold houses are well set back, some around a green, with flower-filled gardens and old stone roofs. No one could build a village like this today and make it look so natural.

The church is tall and spired, though parts of the original Norman work can still be seen, after the various restorations. Close by is a fine manor house built in the 17th Century, altered later but consistently the seat of the Whitmore family until 1964. In the grounds is a splendid old pigeon cote of unusual design.

Upper Slaughter has a Norman church, perhaps built even earlier, but much rebuilt in the Middle Ages and later, using the original

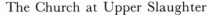

The Church at Upper Slaughter

Norman stonework as building material, making it rather a puzzle today. It was also once the site of a castle, only the mound remaining today, right in the centre of the village. This was also probably built in Norman times but could not have been very large.

Some of the cottages in this little village have the honour of being rebuilt by Sir Edwin Lutyens. A mile to the north lies Eyford Park, a beautiful estate with a large manor house built in 1910, with Rockcliff House close by, the dower house of an earlier manor, restored fairly recently. Close by is the site of a Roman villa, and there are several good examples of barrows and tumuli within a mile or two.

From the narrow country lane joining the two villages, an excellent view of Upper Slaughter Manor is obtained. It is one of the best of all the Cotswold manor houses, dating in part from the 15th Century, with an Elizabethan front. It makes a pretty scene across the fields.

Below the junction with the Dikler, the Windrush meanders quietly for several miles through the fields of a broad valley, with only one bridge across it and no villages at all before Windrush itself, which is built up on the hillside above the south bank. There are mill weirs in the river here and a particularly attractive old mill, built in the 17th Century, still standing by the water, though not in use today.

Windrush has one of the finest Norman churches in the Cotswolds,

Upper Slaughter Manor House

built in the 12th Century and not too much restored and altered later. The south doorway is particularly famous for its beak-heads and saw-tooth decorations and there are many other Norman features, though the tower is much later and is in two stages. In the churchyard there are some remarkable table tombs, with much ornate decoration.

A mile to the south-west is a small, Iron-age hill fort, clearly seen and quite easy to find. It covers nearly three acres of land and must have been of some importance in pre-Christian days.

Three villages stand up on the hillsides above the "unoccupied" stretch of the Windrush—Clapton to the west, and the two Rissingtons east of the river. Clapton is notable in having one of the smallest churches in the Cotswolds, albeit built in the 12th Century. Its nave is but 30 feet by 13, the chancel only 15 feet by 11, and it can hold less than fifty people. It was an early part of the Evesham Abbey domains. Its most interesting feature seems to be an inscription carved on the

Clapton Church

chancel arch, variously interpreted but apparently to the effect that "whoever shall say an Our Father and Hail Mary three times devoutly kneeling and in person, shall be rewarded then and there with a thousand days." Presumably of life!

Great Rissington has an early English church with a particularly large tower of undoubted Norman origin, with some fine Norman arches, but again has been much altered through the centuries. The Manor House, originally 13th Century, stands close to the church but is mostly much later in style now, having been greatly enlarged and rebuilt in 1929.

Little Rissington, a mile or more north, is on a steep hill and again is dominated by a Norman church, though it stands slightly apart from the village on a spur of the hill. An unusual feature is a rare rood-loft staircase beside the chancel arch, built in the 15th Century. The tower here is short and unusually small. Miraculously, this old village has remained virtually unchanged by the proximity of the big R.A.F. airfield just above it on the hill top, but mercifully out of sight. An old corn mill still stands on the river below the village.

While we are on to the Rissingtons, we should mention one more—Wyck Rissington, also on the hillside but above the Dikler this time. It is only a mile north of Little Rissington, though a little difficult to get at. It has a church with a massive Norman tower, out of all proportion but very magnificent just the same. Part of the base may well be Saxon, as also may other small parts of the church. The choir is particularly interesting and unusual in a variety of ways, not least the windows and a stone bench all round the sides. The font is pure Norman though not the base it stands on.

Curiously, it was in this church that Gustav Holst received his first professional engagement, as organist, in 1895, when he was seventeen.

To return to Windrush village again, the river turns eastwards here and soon reaches the two Barringtons, Great on the north and Little on the south.

Great Barrington is a small village, well hidden amidst the trees of Barrington Park, a widespread deer park of great beauty and long the ancestral home of the Bray family. Their connection ended in 1734, but the Norman church, much restored a century and a half later, contains a number of sculptured memorials of the family. The original Manor House was sold by the Bray family to the Lord Chancellor, Lord Talbot, but unfortunately burnt down a year or so later, and little remains of it. The splendid present-day mansion stands close to the same site.

31

Great Barrington Church
32

The church must have been of some considerable size originally. The chancel arch, pure Norman, is far bigger than would be required for the present building. The tower is still largely Norman, despite extensive rebuilding in 1511 and the re-use of much of the original Norman stonework.

The deer park was created by Lord Talbot soon after he bought the estate, while the new Palladian Mansion, the present building, was being erected. It overlooks the Windrush from a terrace, the course of the river having been changed to form a small lake. Various small buildings, some designed as temples, adorn the park.

A particularly fine little bridge crosses the Windrush to Little Barrington, spread out on the slopes above the river. The church here is again Norman, though much smaller, but containing more of the original Norman work, especially the door and arches inside.

Old stone quarries at Great Barrington and Taynton, the next village nearby on the same bank, produced particularly good quality stone, so good indeed, that it was in great demand from far and wide. Several of the Oxford Colleges are built of it, as well as Blenheim Palace and even parts of St. Paul's Cathedral.

A corner of Taynton Quarries

Taynton quarries are known to have been in continuous operation since Saxon times, as long as nine hundred years ago. The Romans before them are also believed to have quarried this stone. The Normans were quick to realise the special quality of Taynton stone, so that we find it in many of the surrounding Cotswold churches. Sir Christopher Wren used large amounts of Taynton stone in his London churches; much of it is recognisable in Saint Paul's Cathedral today, including some of the columns. He also took from Taynton, Thomas Strong as his Master Mason.

Nearly every church in Oxford, including the Cathedral, is made from Taynton stone, Freestone as it is called. Blenheim Palace, which took over twenty years to build, is said to have absorbed two hundred thousand tons of this stone, the best quality that ever came out of the famous quarries. Here Vanbrugh employed as his Master Mason, Valentine Strong, son of Thomas Strong.

A Taynton land-owner, Mr. Philip Lee, living in the village, still operates the quarries on a small scale. We went up to look at them, employing a friendly little boy who offered to be our guide. They are not traditional quarries—great gashes in a hill-side—but rather wide pits out of which the stone is dug. For miles around, it seemed, to judge by the grassed-over heaps of earth, these excavations had been made. Some were open, quite deep holes in which lay exposed large blocks of stone, with crude cranes above and steel chisels and spikes on or embedded in the rock, to split it into suitable blocks. It must be all hand work, with little mechanisation, even today.

But we have now crossed into Oxfordshire, and before we pursue the Windrush through that beautiful county to its confluence with the Thames, we had better return upstream to just above the village of Windrush to explore another important tributary, the Sherborne Brook. This quite sizeable little stream rises near Salperton and could so easily have slipped over the escarpment above Cheltenham and flowed into the Severn. But it trickles gently, with various branches soon coming in, on both sides, to swell its waters to a respectable stream by the time it nears Farmington and turns due east.

Salperton has a small Norman church with many later additions. The nearby park contains a fairly large house, originally 17th Century but much altered and enlarged in 1817.

Turkdean is the next village, up above the stream on the eastern bank. Its original Norman church has been much rebuilt, first in the 15th Century, when much of the Norman stonework was used over again so that only the chancel arch remains pure Norman today. Turkdean Manor, originally late 16th Century and restored early this century, is a particularly fine old house with many mullioned windows.

Our growing stream now passes under the Roman road, Fosse Way, and turns south to Farmington, though not quite reaching this pretty village with its broad green and noble trees. St. Peter's Church at Farmington was early Norman, though enlarged at times from the 13th Century onwards. The south doorway, beneath a much later porch, is a particularly fine example of Norman work.

There is a splendid example of a long barrow just west of the village, and the ancient British fort known as Norbury Camp stands just to the north across the country lane.

From Farmington, a pretty wooded lane winds down to the river again and along to Sherborne itself. This is a long, rather straggling village of Cotswold houses, some with particularly long gardens, opposite the big estate known as Sherborne Park.

The village is in two parts, on either side of the park gates, the eastern end having been largely rebuilt in the early 1800's as a model village. One building, known as The Cottage, curiously enough contains much stonework that was once a Norman church, with two late Norman doorways, though how this came about is not known.

The church almost adjoins the big house and is no older than the late 13th Century, again with many alterations since then.

Sherborne House or Manor was originally built by Thomas Dutton in the mid-16th Century and parts of it can still be seen, though much rebuilding has taken place since then, especially in 1830. Today it is a school, after long years as the seat of the Sherborne family. The park is extensive, some 300 acres, and well wooded, but not normally open to the public. A mile below the village, Sherborne Brook runs into the Windrush and helps to swell its waters.

Taynton, noted, as we have seen, for its famous old quarries, is the first Windrush village in Oxfordshire, and a particularly pretty one, with its church and manor house and old stone roofs. It stands a little above the river which hereabouts is not approached too closely with buildings of any kind, for it is liable to flooding in wet weather. In summer-time, the valley is lush with good grass and wild flowers, where cattle fatten and produce rich milk. In winter it can be under water hundreds of yards wide, often with swans and wild ducks floating on its surface, the river's course quite lost for the time being.

A quieter road than the one through Taynton runs along the south bank of the river closer to the water. Both lead to Burford, one of the

Sherborne House

larger Cotswold towns, and one of the most perfect. It is remarkable that a town so large has not been spoilt by "improvements" but has retained its truly Cotswold character from the top end of its High Street, all the way down the long hill to the old bridge at the bottom, and into the various streets on either side.

Burford, as the name implies, was a place where the river was shallow enough to be crossed by means of a ford. It became important as a road junction in pre-Norman times, yet curiously the Romans never made anything of it, preferring to cross the Windrush at Asthall and Bourton-on-the-Water, on Akeman Street and Fosse Way respectively.

Earliest records indicate that a small settlement existed at the ford early in the 7th Century. But this site was on the western edge of the Kingdom of Mercia, a scene of frontier skirmishing. In 752, the King

Norman doorway, Burford Church

37

of Wessex and his men attacked in force, the battle taking place up on the hill in what is now a playing field known as the "Thirty Acres". The Mercians were defeated but there seems to be no record of what happened to Burford then.

Later, Burford became a great wool centre, with many rich merchants and considerable industry. Its church, originally Norman, as evidenced by its west door and part of its tower, was greatly enriched by the wool merchants in the Middle Ages, like other Cotswold churches, and is now quite an outstanding building, if somewhat mixed in architectural styles. Various chapels were added over the centuries by rich or titled families, and these were indeed burial chambers for successive members of the families. In one part of the church there stands the ornate tomb of Sir Laurence Tanfield, Chancellor of the Exchequer as we would call him today, for both Queen Elizabeth I and James I.

He acquired the Manor of Burford in 1617, and the great house built on the site of the Priory which had fallen at the time of the Dissolution.

A barrel tomb in Burford churchyard

But he was a decidedly corrupt and greedy character, aided and abetted by his wife. Being a smart lawyer, he succeeded in depriving the citizens of Burford of many rights and privileges which they had won over the centuries since early Norman times. The pair of them became thoroughly hated by one and all, but there was nothing that could be done about the situation. The splendid record of good local government gained by Burford—something unusual in those days—was replaced by the most appalling corruption, lasting for a great many years. But the Manor was later bought by Speaker Lenthall of the Long Parliament and it was his grandson, John, who eventually started to root out the evil by means of a Royal Commission. It lingered on, however, until 1861. Such is the evil that can be perpetrated by one man in high office.

By way of contrast to the grand tombs and chapels in the church, the inscription scratched on the stone font can still be seen:

"Anthony Sedley Prisner 1649"

He was one of Cromwell's prisoners and the church records state that he was forced to watch the execution of three of his fellow prisoners here. His own fate is not known, though he doubtless died as well.

Almshouses, built in 1457 by Richard, Earl of Warwick, known as the King Maker, still stand beside the church.

One of the town's great benefactors in the 16th Century was one Simon Wisdom, or Wysdom. On a fine old house standing close to the bridge, a plaque reads:

SYMON WYSDOM ALDERMAN
THE FIRST FOUNDER OF THE SCHOLE
IN BURFORD GAVE THES TENEMENES
WYTHE OTHER TO THE SAME SCHOLE
IN AN 1577 AND NEWLY REEDYFYED
AND BUYLDED THE SAME IN AN 1576
ALL LAWDE AND PRAYSE BE GEVEN
TO GOD THER FORE   AMEN

This was the origin of the Grammar School for Boys founded in 1571, and it is still operating, though now it is co-educational and has some modern buildings.

The Manor House of Burford, high up on the hill, must have been built in Norman times, for it is recorded that it was visited by King Stephen and later by King John, who was Lord of the Manor, and also by Edward I, Edward III and Richard II. Nothing seems to be known about it after the end of the 14th Century, except that it fell into ruins.

But about a hundred years ago, a fine new house was built on the old foundations by the Faulkner family, and that is the house we see today, with considerable remains of the original building still to be seen. The nearby barn is undoubtedly several hundred years old.

One of the choicest bits of Burford is Sheep Street, with the old Lamb Hotel and the Bay Tree, two pleasant hostelries. Almost across the road are the editorial offices of that famous quarterly, "The Countryman", housed in a beautiful building with a large sloping garden behind, full of flowers and apple trees, a most appropriate setting for a magazine devoted to the British countryside in all its aspects.

Burford Priory, a 13th Century monastery, as already mentioned was demolished during the Dissolution, but the present building seems to have been erected in Elizabethan times with the same stone. It was visited by Queen Elizabeth I, James I and William III, and doubtless

The Bay Tree Hotel, Burford

by both the Charles'. Neglected later, it was restored and is now the house of an Anglican community of women.

The Windrush now wanders along its broad valley past Widford, Swinbrook and Asthall, where Akeman Street, the Roman road, used to cross it but of which there is no sign today. To see this lovely stretch, one must stay on the local country lanes and avoid the busy main road (A-40) just up on the hill to the south.

Asthall village, seen best from the bridge, is a gem, even for the Cotswolds. The church shows various architectural periods quite clearly, from Norman through Early English to more recent times. There are some of those curious box-like tombs again in this churchyard. The manor house is Elizabethan and was once the home of the Speaker of the House of Parliament, Lenthall, in King Charles' time, a famous man who was buried in Burford church and who, as stated, once owned Burford Priory.

Swinbrook is a larger village, built up on the hilly northern bank but rather widely scattered. The church is Norman, built around 1200, but the later transformation to Early English is very clear in the nave, with its varied styles in pillars. This is a small church and could not accommodate the large tombs so popular in past centuries. But the Fettiplace family, owners of Swinbrook for a long period, compromised by having effigies laid on shelves on the north wall of the chancel, a most unusual arrangement, carried out in the early 17th and 18th Centuries.

The Redesdale family moved from Asthall to Swinbrook around 1920 and did much good work in the church. Unity Mitford, and more recently Nancy Mitford, the famous Redesdale daughters, are both buried, side by side, in the churchyard.

Swinbrook House, the Fettiplace home, was a fine Elizabethan mansion in its day, yet not a vestige of it now remains. The story goes that it was rented by a Mr. Freeman of London, about 1800. But this worthy gentleman enjoyed the peculiar pastime of highway robbery, inviting guests to his house and robbing them on their way home. He was eventually caught and hanged. The house was then left to decay. It was pillaged from top to bottom and the stones totally removed, doubtless as a ready source of building material.

The hamlet of Widford is notable particularly for its lovely little church set among trees. Quite small, it contains a massive carved wood pulpit. The church was probably built on the site of a Roman villa, for there are small areas of mosaic pavement in the chancel.

41

Effigies in Swinbrook Church

42

When exploring such a peaceful valley as that of the Windrush, it is a pity to use busy main roads. So we will keep to the little lane from Swinbrook to Asthall Leigh and turn right there for Minster Lovell. Turn left again on reaching the quaint old Swan Inn and go to the end of the main street, past some lovely Cotswold houses.

Minster Lovell contains not only a fine big church, with a great tower, above the Windrush, but some splendid ruins of a once large Manor House close beside the water. A beautiful alabaster tomb with an excellent 15th Century effigy, believed to be that of William Lovell, seventh Baron Lovell of Tichmarsh, who built both the church and the manor house, stands in the south transept. A Latin inscription to one Henry Heylin, in the church, translates as: "after the return of Charles II, preferred a quiet and dignified life in the country to the racket and ticklish affairs of Court". A man of our time, no doubt!

One must pay a small charge to see the manor house, but it is well worth it. This was certainly not the first manor house to exist on the site, the Lovells having been lords of the manor, or at least owners of the land, probably from the early 12th Century. The village was known merely as Minster, the name Lovell being added late in the 13th Century. The ruins are those of the manor house built by the seventh Lord Lovell, who was a very rich man in his day. He died in 1455.

Minster Lovell ruins and church

His son John cast his lot in with the Lancastrians in the War of the Roses and was greatly rewarded by Henry VI. But Francis, John's son, had different ideas and became a Yorkist, being created a Viscount by Richard III, thus becoming a man of great power. However, after the defeat of Bosworth Field, he had to flee to Flanders.

The tragic story is told of how he later returned secretly to the Manor, where he hid in a vault or enclosed room and was fed and served by a faithful servant. But the servant met with an accident and thus the ninth baron starved to death in his hide-out. In 1708, during alterations to a chimney, the secret vault was discovered, with a skeleton sitting at a table. It crumbled to dust immediately and was never identified.

After many changes, the manor was bought by Sir Edward Coke, whose descendants became Earls of Leicester. When Holkham Hall, seat of the Leicesters in Norfolk, was built about 1747, the manor house at Minster Lovell was partly demolished and deserted, thus becoming a ruin. It came into the hands of the Ministry of Works in 1935. Today it is yet another splendid example of the restoration work carried out by the Ministry, for the ruins were crumbling and almost entangled with brambles and bushes after so many years of neglect. Now they have mellowed again and one can detect something of the magnificence of the original building. The banks of the river here are lined with big willow trees, through which one can frame the building from various angles.

In the farmyard close by stands a good example of the round stone dovecotes that were such an important feature of the Cotswolds in days gone by.

Pigeon cote at Minster Lovell

Barely two miles down-stream, we now come to the busy little town of Witney, long famous for its blankets. But this is no Burford, with its unspoilt Cotswold style. Here are many modern buildings, a big market in the wide main street and a number of hotels. One has to look for the truly Cotswold features, one of which is the Buttercross, near the church at the top of the main street, a perfect example of a mediaeval market cross, though altered at times in more recent years.

The church has a high steeple but a fine Norman porch on the north side. It must have been rebuilt almost out of recognition since Norman times but contains a number of items of minor interest.

It is possible that the wool industry of Witney goes right back to Roman times. Certainly it was flourishing in the 12th Century, the mills powered by the Windrush, quite a sizeable stream by now and swift flowing.

The blanket industry was brought together and organised into a Company in 1711 by Queen Anne. From then on, all blankets had to be taken to the Blanket Hall, still standing in the High Street, to be checked and weighed. Modern machinery made this routine too cumbersome a century later and the Blanket Weaver's Company was dissolved in 1847. Today, the blanket industry still thrives. Quality has been maintained and Witney blankets are rightly famous throughout the world. Queen Elizabeth II was presented with a pair, embroidered with the Witney coat of arms, in 1960, to commemorate the birth of Prince Andrew.

The lovely Windrush river now really passes out of the Cotswold country, so we will leave it there. It continues to flow peacefully on to its confluence with the Thames some eight or nine miles to the south, splitting into two streams which flow nearly parallel for some miles. It has been a wonderful journey following this river with its rustic sounding name, and we have seen much of the beautiful Cotswold country along its course.

CHAPTER III

Following the Escarpment—To Cheltenham

The Cotswold Hills start some eight miles east of Evesham, with Meon Hill as an outcrop, and just to the south of it, the hills around the Hidcote villages. These are the gentle, rolling hills, but are quite definitely part of the solid block of high ground known as the Cotswolds, which stretches all the way south-westwards to Wotton-under-Edge, some forty miles away in a straight line. But the roads and lanes and steep hills we shall use to explore this lovely region will be far more than forty miles in length, especially when we include all the tempting side-tracks and reversals up and down hills that we shall use to thoroughly observe and discover this unique and largely unspoilt area.

These northerly hills descend gradually to the Gloucester Plain and we have to travel further south-westwards before we come to anything like an escarpment. But even by the time we reach Broadway, less than ten miles away, the hills above this famous village are quite steep and lofty, rearing up nearly eight hundred feet into the sky. The further we progress along this edge of the Cotswolds, the steeper the escarpment becomes, and the more spectacular the views from it, westwards and northwards to the lowlands and the Severn Valley below. Around Stroud we shall find ourselves among really broken hills, with deep valleys and very steep slopes.

All the way along this edge there are villages and small towns, some on the edge, some a little way in from it and others down below at the foot of the hills. And there are some fine old estates and manor houses, with lovely wooded parks, with churches dating back to Norman and even Saxon times, with here and there an abbey or monastery. Scattered widely all over this Cotswold region there are ancient British camps, tumuli and burial barrows, some going back to thousands of years before Christ.

46

The Gloucestershire Plain and the Malverns from the Escarpment

In the early days of ancient Britain, this seems to have been a well settled area. Perhaps it lends itself to being settled, for we find that it did not take the Normans long to spread into these green hills, at that time well forested, and to build their beautiful churches with their characteristic rounded arches and big square towers. And as we have seen, the Romans before them swept inland all over the Cotswolds, building their long straight roads and making the River Severn, for many years, their frontier with the wild region of Wales and the war-like Silures. So there is plenty of history in these Cotswold Hills and not a small part of it lies along the escarpment.

Chipping Campden is a good place to start this part of our exploration. It is a long-established market town, with a very famous market hall, set up a little above the level of High Street. The hall was built in 1627 by Sir Baptist Hicks, a great benefactor of the town. He had bought the manor in 1610 and was one of a number of men, probably most of them wealthy wool merchants, who were responsible for building up the great church, one of the largest and finest of the Cotswold wool churches. Few names are known except that of Hicks, who was an ancestor of the Earls of Gainsborough, but the improvements and building up of the church took place over two hundred years, starting in the 14th Century, the work of many men.

The Market Hall, perhaps the best known building in the town, was intended for the sale of poultry, butter and cheese, and it still bears the

Chipping Campden Market Hall

The Gainsborough Chapel in Chipping Campden Church
49

Hicks coat of arms. But Chipping Campden was a great market town from a much earlier time, especially for the buying and selling of wool, an important export in those days. It is recorded that even in the middle of the 13th century there was a weekly market, as well as several fair days each year. The Market Place is really part of the High Street, quite broad for the most part, with a grassy bank on one side.

The church is large enough to be a cathedral, mostly perpendicular in style and remarkably uniform. This is because it has been most fortunate in its restorers and those who built it up, largely in the 15th Century. Originally late Norman, one has to look long and closely now to find much of the original fabric. But never mind. The rebuilding and expanding were so well done that it is, undoubtedly, one of the most distinguished churches in the whole of the Cotswolds. Even subsequent work and restorations have been carried out with an eye to the whole effect and little if anything has been spoilt. Both the pulpit and the lectern were donated by Hicks before 1620. There are various mortuary chapels, monuments and tombs to dignitaries in the 16th and 17th Centuries, including the inimitable Hicks, so closely associated with the Gainsborough family.

Chipping Campden is most fortunate in having had for many years, a body of residents who were determined to preserve the character of this lovely old town. In 1929, the Campden Trust was formed for the purpose of buying and restoring certain buildings which needed attention, and in general making sure that everything possible was done to preserve the harmony and structure of the town as a whole. Even council houses have been built with Cotswold stone—much more expensive than brick—and so do not intrude on the older buildings.

One could walk leisurely through the town with a good guide book and look out the most interesting buildings. They are well scattered and many have an interesting history, too long to detail here. In the book "English Social History", none other than G. M. Trevelyan declares that the High Street of this town is "the most beautiful village street in England." The Campden Trust deserves much of the credit for this commendation.

All over the town there are fine houses built by the wealthy wool merchants as far back as the 14th Century. One, near the end of Church Street, was the home of William Grevel, and if you look for his brass on the chancel floor of the great church, you will find him described as "The Flower of the wool merchants of all England". He died in this town in 1401, having contributed largely to beautifying the town and restoring the church. Sir Baptist Hicks, who became the first Viscount Campden, also built some fine alms-houses, still in existence, and a large mansion for himself, both near to the church. The house was destroyed during the Civil War and little remains now but the gateway and two gate houses.

From Chipping Campden, it is only a few miles north to Hidcote Boyce and Hidcote Bartrim, with the famous Hidcote Manor between them, and the village of Ebrington a couple of miles south-east. Meon Hill can be seen framed in some of the fine trees hereabouts, especially from a hill called Ilmington Down. Hidcote Manor is most famous for its beautiful gardens, laid out around 1907 by Laurence Johnstone, an American, and now open to the public inder the National Trust. There is some fine topiary and a delightful wooded dell, with many rare plants growing in the shelter of the steep banks and the many trees and bushes. Much original botanical work has been done at Hidcote, and a number of plants now contain the name Hidcote. The manor itself

Almshouses at Chipping Campden

is a mixture of 17th and 18th Century work and fits well into the spacious grounds.

Now to start our long run along the edge of the escarpment, or as near to it as we can keep, we had better descend by narrow lanes to Mickleton, the northernmost Cotswold village. It is just in Gloucestershire; Meon Hill, so close by, is in Warwickshire. It has a late Norman church, enlarged and changed through the ensuing centuries, as in so many cases, but with quite a lot of original Norman work still to be seen. The Manor House is now St. Hilliard's School.

We could travel on the A-46 to Broadway, passing through Aston-sub-Edge and Weston-sub-Edge, with views of the budding escarpment, as these names indicate, on our left. But a more interesting route is up B-4081, nearly to Chipping Campden again, straight on by a country lane that bends round to descend to Willersey, described by H. J. Massingham as:

"Proper Cotswold. Bell Inn, duckpond, barn church with its nice, square dump of a four-pinnacled tower and true old barn-houses are grouped around the green like casual knots of worthies delivering cross-gossip or weather-lore through the slow process of the years." (From "Wold Without End" by H. J. Massingham).

At Willersey we find a Norman church, with a fine big perpendicular tower, built in the 15th Century, containing a peal of six bells, cast in the year 1712. The metal came from three big bells already hanging in the tower. The people of Willersey decided that they wanted more merry bell-ringing, hence the change. A filled-up Norman door can be seen on the south side of the church, the font is pure Norman and the pillars and arches are 13th Century. The great tower rises from the middle of the church on sturdy pillars and magnificent arches, quite remarkable for a village church. On Willersey Hill, above the village, stands a large Iron Age fort.

Before descending to Willersey there are views of Dover's Hill, a mile or so north-west of Chipping Campden, with vast panoramas from the hill, which is a fine vantage point. Today it is National Trust property and is a favourite site for picnics and days in the country. The Trust has built a sizeable car park and there are splendid walks all along the edge of the hills.

Dover's Hill is named after Robert Dover, who inaugurated the Cotswold Games there, around 1650, sometimes known as the Olympick Games. He was evidently a great country gentleman, a retired lawyer with a sporting spirit, a keen horseman and a public benefactor. He caught the King's ear, through a friend in Court, and the King not only approved the scheme but, so it is said, actually gave Dover some of his old clothes, to dress up performers in the games and give them a truly royal air.

Horse-riding, coursing and cock-fighting were always popular at the Sports, and also the particularly Cotswold sport of shin-kicking, where village vied with village. H. J. Massingham, in his famous book, describes this painful game in some detail. It was two full centuries before these games were finally stopped because of the rowdy crowds who assembled on Dover's Hill by the mid-19th Century, but they were revived in 1951 for the Festival of Britain.

Near Willersey is another little Cotswold village that must not be missed on any account—Saintbury. It stands some way up the escarpment alone, with part Saxon—part Norman church on a bluff overlooking the plain, with the outcroppings of the Cotswolds standing out boldly in the distance. The village is strangely scattered, with hardly any two houses on the same level. The church stands all alone, and is surprisingly full of architectural treasures spanning many centuries, not least being the Saxon dial. William Latimer was vicar here, friend of Sir Thomas More and translator of the New Testament. Somewhere in the little churchyard it is believed that his remains lie buried.

Now we come to Broadway, spurned by some because it has become too popular. Certainly it is often crowded in summer-time and at week-ends in the Spring and Autumn. But the secret is to see it first thing in the morning, or late on a summer's evening when the crowds are not there. Then it turns out indeed to be a gem of lovely old stone houses and little shops, set well back from the road across the grassy swards. True, not all is perfect. It has paid the penalty of being wooed too often and by too many, but it is really surprisingly intact and much of its original beauty is unspoilt.

We can reach Broadway quickly from Saintbury or Willersey on the main road, A-46, or we can climb up the escarpment and descend to the village by Fish Hill. As we shall have a lot to explore on the hills, I suggest that we keep to the lower road. We come into the town about halfway along the famous main street and here we must stop and wander about on foot for a while. Broadway has so many little corners, groups of cottages, flower-filled gardens, sometimes flowing out over the greensward, lovely doorways, quaint little shops and so on, that one would miss them nearly all, except on foot.

The Lygon Arms, a truly first-class hotel, is an historical building with a

53

The font at Saintbury Church

huge and beautiful garden of utter peace and beauty hidden from the road. Known as the White Hart until 1820, the Lygon Arms was first built around the end of the 15th Century and has been added to at intervals ever since, always in good taste. It is believed that both Charles I and Cromwell stayed there.

Behind the front of the Lygon Arms there is a courtyard so large that the North Cotswold Hunt gathers there each autumn, before streaming out—all horses, pink coats and yelping fox hounds—through the arch into the main street and out onto the wolds in search of foxes. Truly a wonderful sight, a real bit of old England.

The parish church is quite modern and not nearly so interesting as St. Eadburgha's Church, on the edge of the village along the road to Snowshill. This must have been the original Broadway Church and it truly looks its part, with its square tower and well-proportioned building half hidden among the trees. Like so many Cotswold churches, it goes back many centuries and was doubtless originally Norman, though little remains now that is any earlier than the 15th Century. Curiously, this church has no stained glass windows.

Across the road is a large house known as Middle Hill, at one time the home of Sir Thomas Phillips, the great book collector of all time. He was born in 1792 and began by buying up old vellum documents which were being destroyed and lost. Gold beaters, for instance, still use old vellum in beating out gold metal to the thinness required for gilding statues and furniture, a highly skilled business. Phillips was horrified to see these old documents being lost in this and other ways, and so he bought as many as he could. His collecting went on to include both manuscripts and books, becoming virtually a mania, so that soon Middle Hill was literally full of books. It became almost impossible to even get along the corridors.

Sir Thomes was a wealthy man and he bought up whole libraries, not only in Britain, but very much on the Continent, from big houses and even churches and monasteries. He was able to acquire some unique treasures in France after the Napoleonic Wars. But he did not know when to stop. Despite his great wealth, he overspent on several occasions and had to stay abroad for long periods so that his creditors could not lay hands on him. But his resources always caught up and he eventually moved to Thirlestane House in Cheltenham, in 1857, where there was more room and where he lived for his last fifteen years.

After his death in 1872, the family began to sell off this, the greatest private book collection in the history of the world, fortunately in a

Meeting of the Hunt at the Lygon Arms Hotel, Broadway

Broadway Beacon, on Broadway Hill

highly professional manner. Eventually the large residue of the collection was bought by the Robinson brothers, of Pall Mall, and they have continued to sell off these literary treasures over many years, right up to the present day, largely through big sales at Sotheby's.

The main road from Evesham (A-44) is the one which runs right along the main street of Broadway and up the escarpment by means of a series of great bends at quite a steep gradient, soon plunging into dense beech-woods on either side. It is a pity there is usually so much traffic on this hill and nowhere to stop to admire the views. Here, surely, is a hill on which there should be a stopping place, so that travellers may pull off the road to rest and absorb some of the beauties of the Cotswolds. By the time one has reached the little Fish Inn at the top, the view has disappeared. But the situation can be retrieved and indeed improved at the expense of a little time.

Just beyond the Fish Inn, there is a road on the right to Snowshill. Half a mile along it, there is a broad parking place opposite the entrance to Broadway Tower, on the highest part of the hill, here known as Broadway Beacon. Here, untroubled by noise and traffic you may spend as long as you like, admiring one of the finest views in England. Pray for a fine clear day and you may well see not only Bredon Hill, which is comparatively near, but the Malvern Hills beyond, and the Forest of Dean away to the left. On the clearest day, it is possible to see far into Wales and up the Welsh Marches, with Tewkesbury and other towns and villages scattered everywhere.

The tower was built by the Earl of Coventry, in the late 1700's, to please his wife, who wanted to be able to see it from the family seat near Worcester. It is said that Rosetti, William Morris and Burne-Jones used to spend holidays here, finding it rather a bind carrying their food all the way up the hill from Broadway. The lane past the tower is part of Buckle Street, the Roman road known as Ryknild Street, which runs almost due north and south. If we follow it back to the main road again, cross A-44 and carry on, we shall soon be among the hills above Saintbury and Willersey again, a lovely stretch of country that could well absorb an afternoon or even a whole day, away from crowds, perhaps with a picnic lunch to be enjoyed in some delectable setting.

But let us carry on to Snowshill, along the top of the escarpment, a secluded hill village with a lovely Tudor mansion known as Snowshill Manor, now in the care of the National Trust. The Manor was originally given to the Abbey of Winchcombe by Kenulf, the King of Mercia, in the year 821. At the Dissolution of the monasteries, Henry

Snowshill Manor

VIII gave it to his wife, Catherine Parr. The present house was built around 1500 but has been altered at various times since. The interior is filled with thousands of items from days gone by, a most unusual museum of furniture, musical instruments, arms and scientific instruments of a wide variety, as well as an enormous collection of craft tools of great interest.

All this is the work of Mr. Charles Wade, who bought the Manor in 1919 and restored it at considerable expense. Ugly out-buildings were removed and the present beautiful terraced gardens laid out. Wade was another inveterate collector, and the Manor was soon filled with his vast and varied collection. He gave it all to the National Trust in 1951, and they are preserving it exactly as it was, cluttered collection and all, just as the owner would wish. He died in 1956, at the age of 73. The

The bell-ringer at Snowshill Manor

Manor is also the site of one of the large Cotswold pigeon cotes.

The church at Snowshill, St. Barnabas, was built only in 1864, in 13th Century style, with very thick walls. But stone carving that should have been executed was never done and the whole effect leaves much to be desired. However, it sits well amidst the lovely cottages with their flower-filled gardens on the steep hillside. When a group of round barrows half a mile away were excavated, some outstanding graves were found, producing one item at least, the famous Snowshill Dagger, which is now in the British Museum.

We can now carry on along the road to Ford, on the infant Windrush, but here we must make a sharp right turn and run down Stanway Hill to see a few of the exquisite little villages below the escarpment. The first is Stanway itself, named doubtless from Stane Way, an ancient road which climbs straight up into the hills here. We have just descended by newer road, with fine views almost all the way down.

Stanway has a beautiful Manor House with a magnificent gateway, through which one may peep at the front of the house. The manor was part of the domains of the Abbey of Tewkesbury for nearly a thousand years, but was bought by the Tracy family in the 16th century, and it was they who built the original manor house. Later, it became the seat of the Earl of Wemyss and in the ensuing years it has been altered on various occasions, though certainly not spoilt. The elaborate gateway was probably built about 1630, though not by Inigo Jones, as is often claimed. It is set at right-angles to the main house and greatly enhances it.

In the grounds of Stanway House, as it is called, is a 15th Century tithe barn, a really fine example of a Cotswold barn, now used for social gatherings. Close beside the great gateway is the church, probably originally Norman but now so mutilated with periodical changes that it is of no special interest, though its lovely mellow stone matches well that of the manor house. Its fame is redeemed somewhat, however, by the fact that in the graveyard is buried the physician Thomas Dover, who introduced mercury into medicine.

There is a delightful winding country lane joining Stanway to Stanton, a couple of miles away, and surely one of the prettiest of all the Cotswold villages. How fortunate that it is not on a main road! Here it lies, quiet and peaceful, the very epitome of the perfect country village, totally unspoilt, it seems. Massingham, that great lover of the Cotswolds, describes it so aptly as: "many gabled Stanton, drawn in

Stanway House, Stanway

The village of Stanton

63

under the ankles of the wolds." And indeed it is, right at the foot of the escarpment, with the hills soaring up, tree-laden, from the end of the main street.

There is a track up the steep hill at the end of the village, incredibly a coach road some three centuries back, leading up to Snowshill, nearly a thousand feet above sea level and only a couple of miles away. Only one mile away, on the very edge of the hill, stands the remains of Shenberrow, a large Iron Age fort covering nearly five acres.

Stanton is a village built almost entirely of Cotswold stone in the 16th and 17th Centuries, and it can have altered but little since then. Doubtless most of the houses and cottages have been modernised, but succeeding generations must have made quite sure that nothing was going to spoil the outward look of their village, come what may.

Much of the credit in recent times must certainly go to Sir Philip Stott, himself an architect, who bought the estate containing the village in 1906 and did a lot of restoring in the most careful manner. He died in 1937; the lovely village today is his memorial.

The church is Perpendicular in style, with a tall spire, all nicely tucked away among noble trees, but it started out as a late Norman church and there are still bits of original Norman work to be seen in it. There are traces of 14th Century wall paintings, and two pulpits in the church, even some 15th Century glass, although it seems that this came from Hailes Abbey, only a few miles away.

Buckland lies a little to the north-east, part of the way up on the hills, but unless we are going to tramp across the wooded slopes, we must go down to the main road (A-46) and turn up the lane to this secluded little village, with no way beyond it. Its Early English church contains the finest 15th Century glass in all the Cotswolds, again rescued from Hailes Abbey at the time of the Dissolution. Two other treasures consist of a former altar frontal of exquisite 15th Century needlework, and the Buckland Bowl, of wood and silver, thought to be at least 15th Century and in continual use ever since then. It is one of the rewards of exploring remote villages to come across so many treasures in one tiny place.

Now we must turn south again and follow the main road to the turning on the left for Hailes Abbey, two miles beyond Stanway. Only ruins today, fine though they are, set deep in the hills, this was once a flourishing Abbey, built by Richard, Earl of Cornwall, the brother of Henry III, as a thanks-offering for being delivered safely from a great storm off the Scilly Isles. It was completed in 1253 but was actually

Hailes Abbey ruins near Winchcombe

dedicated two years earlier, with Henry III and his Queen, many bishops and hundreds of knights present. In 1270, the second Earl of Cornwall presented a phial believed to contain some of the blood of Our Lord, vouched for by the Pope and the Patriarch of Jerusalem. This drew vast crowds of pilgrims to Hailes Abbey for many years, when on special occasions the phial was brought out on display from its shrine, and miracles were said to have occurred.

In 1539, at the time of the Dissolution, all the splendour of this great Abbey was brought to the ground and totally destroyed. Its treasures were scattered, the holy phial was declared to be a fake, and even the lead roofs were taken away to London for other uses by the King. Only the house of the Abbot was spared. And all this was done by Bishop Latimer of Worcester, such was the vast change wrought by Henry

VIII in the then Church of England.

We are indebted to the National Trust, and the former Ministry of Works, for the present appearance of these abbey ruins. They were received as a gift in 1936 and the Trust and the Ministry have done a splendid job of clearing and partly restoring at least the foundations and some arches of the great buildings. The Museum is particularly good and gives one a fair idea of what the abbey must have looked like in its prime.

Hailes Church, close to the Abbey, was built long before the Abbey, around 1130, in Norman times. Some parts of the original building can still be seen, evidently having survived the destruction of the nearby Abbey. Some tiles and other items undoubtedly came from the Abbey.

A narrow road, known as Salter's Way, will take us up on to Salter's Hill and Sudeley Hill, above the abbey ruins, with splendid views along the edge of the hills northwards, and down on to Sudeley Castle and its park, with the little town of Winchcombe just beyond. A few miles to the west, the great bulk of Cleeve Hill stands like a barrier defending Cheltenham, below it on the far side.

On Cleeve Hill above Cheltenham

Sudeley Castle has had a very unstable history of owners. Originally built in the reign of King Stephen, it was occupied and rebuilt by Ralph Boteler in the first half of the 15th Century. At his death, it was seized by the Crown. From then on, it seems to have been in and out of royal hands a number of times. In 1547, King Edward VI gave it to Lord Admiral Seymour who, in that year, married Catherine Parr, widow of Henry VIII. They had been secret lovers for some time, but unfortunately she died a year after the marriage, in childbirth. Her tomb lies in the chapel attached to the Castle.

Seven years later, Sudeley Castle was given to the Chandos family, but was badly damaged at the time of the Civil War and not restored until well into the 19th century, by the Dent family. Around 1854, Sir Gilbert Scott was involved in the work. This restoration took nearly a century and was only completed in the early 1930's by J. H. Dent-Brocklehurst. Today, the castle and grounds are open to the public at specific times but not on all days. It is very well worth seeing, set as it is amidst beautiful wooded hills at the foot of the escarpment.

Winchcombe is one of the most perfect and typical of all the small Cotswold towns, fitting perfectly into its environment. It is virtually surrounded by rolling hills, with the escarpment as a back-drop and round to the north-east, while Langley Hill, an out-crop from the main range, fills in the north-western sky. Nearly every building is made from the Cotswold stone; houses, inns, and the fine big church.

Winchcombe has an ancient history, reaching back to Saxon times, when it was walled and defended, and the site of a great abbey built in the 8th Century by Kenulf, the King of Mercia. The town was sacked by the Danes, rebuilt in the 11th Century, only to be destroyed by fire again two hundred years later. Once more restored, the abbey remained of great importance but became just one more victim of the Dissolution. In 1539, Lord Seymour of Sudeley was entrusted with the job of utterly destroying this, one of the great abbeys of the country, so that today not a sign of it remains, though there is an Abbey Square in the town.

It seems that in the 16th Century, tobacco was grown locally and much wealth was enjoyed by Winchcombe from this source. But the West Indian tobacco interests were strong enough to have this local industry suppressed, leaving only some of the wealthy merchants' houses as relics of the trade. Apparently wine was another trade then, because to this day there is a Vineyard Street, running partly by the river, where there was a ducking stool, used by husbands to cool off their nagging wives, and occasionally to duck a so-called witch. Out-

A gargoyle on Winchcombe Church

side the Town Hall there are some old stocks, though the building is 19th Century. In the Town Hall is the charter granted by Queen Elizabeth I, permitting the town to have a market and a fair. Some of the old inns are interesting, especially the George, which has a mediaeval gallery, part of a larger one in days gone by.

Winchcombe Church is 15th Century Perpendicular, a combined effort of the then Abbot and the parish, with some help from Sir Ralph Boteler, who also did much work on Sudeley Castle nearby. Much rebuilding has taken place since then but this is indeed one of the big Cotswold churches, not perhaps a true wool church but partly at least a tobacco church, though the wealth from wool undoubtedly played the greater part in its building. It contains certain relics of the old abbey, which have been unearthed at various times since the destruction. A curious feature of this church consists of the large number of particularly grotesque gargoyles adorning the exterior.

One can well imagine that the outstanding spurs of the Cotswold escarpment would make natural sites for ancient British forts, and later for the Roman forts which were built so widely. The remains of two ancient forts can be seen on the hills above and just to the east of Hailes Abbey, one known as Beckbury Camp, from where it is said that Thomas Cromwell watched the destruction of the abbey below.

On Langley Hill and Nottingham Hill and on Cleeve Hill, all just to the west of Winchcombe, were other earthworks and forts, some dating back to pre-Roman times. There are also burial mounds and tumuli on many of the Cotswold Hills.

One of the best of the long whale-back burial mounds stands high above Winchcombe and goes by the curious name of Belas Knap Long Barrow. It stands a thousand feet above sea level and was partly restored by the Ministry of Works in 1931. Little is known of its early history, but it is reliably believed to have been built about four thousand years ago, possibly as early as 2,500 B.C. It belongs to the late Neolithic period and probably remained untouched until Roman times.

Some burial mounds had long central passages, with burial chambers on each side; others had burial chambers entered from the outside, with a false entrance at the wider end, probably to put tomb robbers off the scent. Belas Knap is a good example of the latter, and belongs to the Severn-Cotswold group, as classified by Dr. Glyn E. Daniel, who has done so much research into burial mounds in Britain. The mound is now nearly 180 feet long, with a maximum width of 60

Belas Knap Burial Mound

feet and a height of just over 13 feet. It is believed to have been appreciably longer and wider when first built.

It was originally built of slabs of flat local stone, made into walls running along and across, and with outer walls of the same material, probably among the earliest examples of the dry stone walling that is so common today. It was roofed with large slabs of stone sloping down on either side, and the burial chambers were built from slabs of stone standing upright. During excavations between 1863-1865, a total of thirty skeletons was found in the various chambers, almost all of the long-headed type. Belas Knap is easily reached by a field path from the road to Brockhampton.

Cleeve Hill, the highest of all the Cotswold hills (over 1,000 feet), could well be called the playground of Cheltenham, sheltering so closely down below. Fortunately or not, depending on one's physical condition, there is no road over the hill and the common. But there are various walks up on to the hill, the most popular and crowded, being from the village of Cleeve Hill on the Winchcombe road. A somewhat longer walk, but one with magnificent views virtually all the way along, starts near Charlton Kings, and there are other walks, some along cart tracks, from the eastern side of the hill.

One way to get up to Cleeve Hill by car, nearly to the highest point, is to turn left off the A-40 road, to Whittington, and then left again along a country lane which is sign-posted "Cleeve Common". This comes out at the radio station, and the whole top of the hill is then spread out, with wonderful views and walks everywhere. It is well worth the effort to get up on to Cleeve Hill and Common, especially on a brilliant clear day of sunshine, when half of England seems to be displayed below, not to speak of the Welsh mountains in the distance.

There is a splendid golf course on Cleeve Common, and not far from the Club House, an Iron Age British fort, now scheduled as an ancient monument. Below the camp is a huge slab of rock known as Huddlestone's Table. Tradition has it that this is the spot where King Kenulf of Mercia said farewell to the many guests, royal and otherwise, who attended the dedication of the great abbey of Winchcombe, which he founded in the 8th Century.

Now that we are standing above the rooftops of Cheltenham, it seems an opportune moment to go down and examine this beautiful city. It doubtless arose as a small settlement long ago, because it is a natural road junction. But it was not until about two centuries ago that it really began to grow, when mineral springs were discovered and developed, so that Cheltenham rather suddenly became a well known spa. The event which sealed its fate and prosperity was the visit, in 1788, of King George III with his family. His doctor had advised him to take the Cheltenham waters for the good of his health. Like everyone else, he arose early each morning, took the prescribed glasses of water, and walked about to give himself the exercise which was also said to be so essential to good health. By mutual consent, apparently, it was agreed to drop all ceremony and pomp, he and his family behaving like any other visitors, walking and driving about the town with the crowds.

From then on, everyone who was anyone had to visit Cheltenham. In 1816, the Duke of Wellington himself opened an Assembly Room, and the King declared the theatre to be a Theatre Royal. Famous

The Imperial Gardens, Cheltenham

72

people in every walk of life flocked to this fashionable Spa—Sir Walter Scott, Tennyson and other poets, Mrs. Craik and Margaret Kennedy, Gustav Holst and many famous musicians and actors—all were to be found in Cheltenham during the season. Today it is less important as a spa, but has gained as a seat of learning, with the famous Cheltenham Ladies College, the Boys Grammar School and the Gloucestershire College of Art among its various well known educational establishments.

The centre of the city, and easily the most beautiful part, lies along the Promenade, with the Imperial Gardens ablaze with flowers from Spring to Autumn, the stately Queen's Hotel at the top, and behind it the Montpelier Gardens. On the other side of the Promenade, with its double row of magnificent trees, stand the beautiful stately Georgian terraces which look so exactly right in this environment. It is indeed a beautiful city today, despite its considerable expansion and the inroads of industry in recent decades. It forms an excellent centre for exploring the Cotswolds, if one prefers the comforts and attractions of a city to the delights of a country inn or small hill town.

CHAPTER IV

The Escarpment—Cheltenham to Painswick

Let us go back up into the hills and continue our explorations along the escarpment. We can leave Cheltenham by several roads. One is the Cleeve Hill road, A-46, which goes on to Broadway and Stratford-on-Avon, through Winchcombe. Another is the road through Charlton Kings, A-40, past Andoversford and on to Oxford. A right fork at Charlton Kings, A-435, takes us up to Seven Springs (one source of the Thames) and on down the valley of the Churn to Cirencester. Leckhampton Hill, almost overhanging Cheltenham, leads steeply up on the B-4070 road, to Air Balloon and on A-417 to Birdlip and then on to Cirencester also. The Shurdington road, again A-46, starts off westwards across the plain, then climbs in great sweeps up to Cranham Woods and on to Painswick and Stroud.

To provide continuity to our explorations, we had better take the A-40 road to Andoversford, then turn right along A-436 to Seven Springs. Soon we begin to get some fine views back over the town and far beyond. Immediately after the crossing with the Cirencester road, there is a lay-by behind a clump of trees and here we must stop. Down in a hollow, trickling partly from a sloping stone embankment, seven tiny springs emerge, to create a little stream which promptly passes under the road to form a small lake in a private garden. This is the source of the Thames, the one that is furthest from the mouth, but which is contested by many people, who insist that the true source is at Thameshead, a few miles west of Cirencester. I prefer Seven Springs, and so do many other people.

It is worth descending Leckhampton Hill for a mile or so, to a lane on the right which leads to Salterley Grange Hospital and so up on to the hill itself, where there are more splendid walks. The road on to Air Balloon, once a famous pub at the top of Leckhampton Hill, runs right along through rolling hills, with magnificent views northwards.

74

Seven Springs, the source of the Thames

Birdlip, a tiny hamlet at the top of Birdlip Hill, a long and very steep ascent from the plain far below, stands on the Roman Road known as Ermin Street, running from Gloucester (Glevum) to Cirencester (Corinium in Roman days) and beyond. This is an extremely long, steep hill and one can well believe a staging post for horses was necessary at the top. Such a post existed in Roman times, standing on the spot where the Royal George Hotel stands today, beside the road. Magnificent views can be obtained from Birdlip Hill on the way down.

Our escarpment road runs now through Buckholt Woods, emerging on to the A-46 road after its long climb up from the plains, and close to Prinknash Abbey. This is something quite unique in the Cotswolds,

Gloucestershire Plain from Birdlip Hill

The cloisters of Prinknash Abbey

a monastery of Benedictine monks in their white robes. They came from Caldey Island, off the coast of South Wales in 1928, and have prospered greatly since then, operating a pottery works, farming their land by the most modern methods, and setting up a retreat, with an excellent library, that is now something of a seat of learning. Recently they opened a new abbey on the estate, a magnificent building made from the local Guiting stone, with a beautiful little church at the back, over which the monks hope one day to build a great abbey church This present one will then become the crypt.

But there have been monks at Prinknash since early Norman times. Prinknash itself first seems to have been mentioned in the time of King Alfred, around 890 A.D. It is certainly mentioned in the Domesday Book, when William the Conqueror gave Buckholt, which included Prinknash, to a branch of the Giffards of Brimpsfield, a Norman baronial family which had given substantial help to William during his invasion of England. Osberne Giffard became the Lord of Brimpsfield and it was his son, Heylas, who gave parts of the woods of Buckholt to the Benedictine monks of Gloucester, in 1096. During the next two centuries, the abbey lands were considerably extended, and the monks organised hunting parties for visitors, complete with dogs and huntsmen, in their woods. Apparently the Abbot of Gloucester made Prinknash Abbey his residence about 1525, possibly earlier.

The last Abbot of Gloucester, William Parker, entertained Henry VIII and Anne Boleyn for a week near to Prinknash, though it is not proven that it was in the Abbey itself. Certainly the King hunted on the Prinknash estate, apparently with much pleasure. Fortunately, perhaps, Abbot Parker died some months before King Henry's suppression of the monasteries. In 1540 the Abbey was surrendered and the monks were pensioned off. The King made the county of Gloucester into an episcopal See, with the Abbot of Tewkesbury as the first Bishop of the county. Prinknash Abbey became the country home of the bishop.

The house then had a series of owners during the next few centuries, with much interesting history attached to it. It was the stately home of various families during the 18th and 19th Centuries, some of whom made certain alterations and improvements in their time. In 1888, it was bought by Thomas Dyer Edwardes, who was born some forty years earlier. He made substantial improvements both to the house and the whole estate, including the present long drive from the Stroud road, with two lodges at the gate, and employed many men as gardeners and farm workers to run the estate.

In 1924, this Thomas Edwardes became a Catholic and in the same year, he invited the monks of Caldey Island to come to Prinknash and form a foundation. The following year, when two of the Caldey monks came to take over the property, Mr Edwardes died suddenly on a visit to Naples, making the Deed of Gift inoperative. But his grandson, the 20th Earl of Rothes (through the marriage of his father, the 19th Earl, to Edwardes' daughter, Noel, in 1900) who inherited the estate, immediately had a new Deed of Conveyance made out so that the monks received the gift as his grandfather wished, a noble and generous act.

Later in 1928, the Caldey monks performed the complicated task of moving to Prinknash, and immediately set about converting the manor house into a monastery, no easy job, for there were thirty of them. On Caldey Island, they had been unsuccessful in making their estates a paying proposition, and a Benedictine abbey must be a viable proposition economically. The gift of Prinknash was a blessing indeed, and the monks set about making it a success with great enthusiasm. Their numbers increased steadily as more novices were brought in and trained. They were not short of capital because they had sold the Island of Caldey, together with their monastery on it, to the Cistercians, who are still there and apparently making a success of it.

Despite alterations and additions to the Abbey, and the hiring of overflow accommodation, by 1947 it became necessary to create other foundations. One was at Farnborough Abbey and the second at Pluscarden Priory in Scotland, both interesting places themselves. But even before the Second World War, the Prinknash monks knew that they must have a larger abbey. Great plans were made and the foundation stone was laid in 1939 by Cardinal Hinsley. The war stopped the building but it was resumed afterwards, on a larger scale, and has just recently been finished (1972), though there are plans for considerable additions, including an abbey church, in years to come.

During the early excavations, the monks came upon a bed of high quality clay, and it was this that led to their making pottery on a commercial basis, after much experimentation. This was merely the renewal of an ancient industry, for there is plenty of evidence that pottery was made at Prinknash even in Roman times. The pottery made today by the Prinknash monks is known and valued all over the world, and forms their largest industry. But they also make incense, which is exported widely, as well as iron work, stained glass for windows, religious vestments and various other things. All this is more than they can accomplish themselves, so that today they employ quite a number of workers from the neighbourhood, both in the factory and

79

workshops and on the land as well.

Prinknash Abbey is a thriving organisation indeed, all the profits going into monastic buildings which continue to grow steadily year by year. The original abbey building, the old manor house, is now a rest house and retreat for visitors.

Our route along the Cotswold escarpment now takes us into a region of broken hills, deep winding valleys with a few small industrial towns far down below the surroundings hills, sometimes with flat table-lands above, or rolling hills with much woodland beside the fields and sheep pastures. It is far more rugged and broken country than we have seen so far, yet with a beauty and grandeur that is quite unique. Curiously, this is not tourist country like the rest of the Cotswolds, possibly just because it is industrialised to some extent. Yet the mills and factories rarely spoil the scenery. They are tucked down well out of sight in the valleys, there are no great clouds of smoke or cases of pollution. Indeed, many of the woollen mills are quite attractive, set amidst trees in the most rural settings. And many of them have interesting histories.

Yet tourists do not come to this part of the Cotswolds in any great numbers. There are not many hotels; there are no Broadways or Bourton-on-the-Waters, yet some of the villages are just as pretty. There are some beautiful estates, with fine manor houses, and everywhere churches that go back to Norman times and even earlier. The panoramas from the high hills along the edge are the best in all this hilly region, there are tumuli and burial mounds that were made when Egypt was at the height of its glory, and nearly every hill top has the remains of an Iron Age fort, or one of the series of Roman forts erected all along the edge. It is strange to me that this is not popular tourist country. All the better for those who do discover it; the roads are clearer and there is no congestion at the special beauty spots.

Painswick comes first after Prinknash Abbey, less than three miles away. It is a pretty little town, set upon a spur of high land above one of the many valleys that break up these southern hills. The greatest claim to fame lies in the hundred yew trees which adorn the churchyard, clipped and shaped and beautifully kept at all times. One says a hundred but, in fact, there never have been exactly that number. Today it seems that there are ninety-nine. They were planted nearly two hundred years ago, an exact hundred. But always one or two died; it was said to be the work of the Devil. So more than a hundred were planted and thus the century was always maintained.

The church is now mostly early 15th Century, though it stands on

80

Yews at Painswick Church

81

the site of an earlier Norman, or even Saxon church. To some extent it is another wool church, for many wealthy wool merchants lived in and near Painswick during the great wool years in the 14th and 15th Centuries. It has a tall spire on top of a square tower, and is quite a land-mark all round, especially from a cross-roads known as Bull's Cross, a mile away to the south-east, across the valley.

The church has not enjoyed an altogether peaceful career. The spire has been struck twice by lightning, once in 1763 and again in 1883, when it crashed through the roof of the church, causing great damage. It is also said that, after Charles I failed to capture Gloucester in 1643, some of the Parliamentary troops took refuge in the church and were flushed out with fire and hand grenades, again causing much damage.

Apart from its yew trees, Painswick's churchyard is famous for its many box and pedestal tombs, a quite remarkable collection. John Bryan, a local sculptor, was responsible for many of them. He worked from early in the 18th Century until his death in 1787, but his own is one of the simpler ones among the near hundred tombs which adorn the churchyard today. Some excellent work of restoration has now been going on for some time by local people, thus saving many of the tombs which were falling into decay. They are altogether too good to lose.

There are several outstanding buildings in Painswick, and numerous little streets and corners that are truly Cotswold in character. The old

The main street of Painswick

Court House, close to the church, was built in 1604, as a wool merchant's house. A little to the south stands a house known as Castle Hale, another fine building on the site of a former mediaeval manor house. The Falcon Inn, built in 1711, is famous for its bowling green. Painswick is definitely a place where one leaves the car and wanders round on foot. The main street is quite long and slopes down westwards, with various sideside streets on both sides. It is well worth exploring these, for this is a quiet and peaceful little town, very orderly and well kept.

But it has not always been so peaceful. Henry VIII and Anne Boleyn spent two days here at the time they visited Prinknash, two happy days, it is recorded. Yet a year later she was beheaded in the Tower of London. Charles I came here in 1643, elated that he was about to capture Gloucester, but he returned a few weeks later crestfallen and defeated. Curiously, the son of Anne Boleyn's jailer, Sir Anthony Kingston, was lord of the manor of Painswick, a man of evil and sinister reputation who apparently took pleasure in building a prison at Painswick, now long since forgotten.

If we follow the spur of land upon which Painswick stands, back north-eastwards, we come on to Painswick Hill, or Beacon, with an ancient hill fort on top of it, known as Kimsbury Castle. This is an Iron Age fort enclosing some eight acres, with steep banks and the remains of ditches still well preserved. It commands a magnificent view all round and down across the Severn Valley, ideal as a site for a fort. A golf course covers the rest of the hill.

The Severn Valley from Stanley Wood, near Painswick

CHAPTER V

The Southern Cotswolds

Painswick stands above a valley running down to Stroud, the chief wool town in this part of the country in years gone by. But before we go on to Stroud, let us examine a tangle of lofty hills to the west and south-west of Painswick, separated from the main Cotswold massif except at Painswick Hill, which is a sort of isthmus between the two. I think these hills are perhaps the most beautiful part of all the Cotswolds. There is a wildness and remoteness about them, an isolation and freshness that is quite unmistakable. Much of the land on the hill-tops is in the care of the National Trust but it is all open to the public. There are roads and narrow country lanes running everywhere, but one is bound to get lost, for they wind and twist and can be rather confusing. But this matters little, for it is all such beautiful country and one comes out eventually to the main spots or peaks.

Haresfield Beacon is perhaps the best of the look-out points. It stands high on a steep spur above the Severn Plain and you can see not only southwards along the edge of the escarpment but westwards across the Severn to the Forest of Dean and the Welsh mountains beyond, and north-eastwards along the other edge of the hills towards Cheltenham. Gloucester lies below, only a few miles away. Remains of a Roman or British fort can clearly be seen on this hill, and there are others on nearby peaks.

Another good look-out point is Shortwood Hill, and there are ridge roads which often command beautiful views, though I often felt frustrated here, and on other ridges in the Cotswolds, because there were too many trees. One knows that there are wonderful views just below the road but they cannot be seen through the dense screen of trees. I would like to see more small areas cleared and laid out as parking places, with enough trees removed to enable visitors to see the magnificent panoramas. I am a great tree lover but I feel that a few could be spared here for the benefits that would follow.

The Gloucestershire Plain from Haresfield Hill

Stroud is a busy little town, a jumble of steep hills and narrow streets, a market town and shopping centre for the surrounding country. It is also a scene of considerable industry, though many of the woollen mills now produce other things and some have disappeared altogether. It is no longer a typical Cotswold town, though it has some attractive corners, and some real old Cotswold houses here and there. The Town Hall, in the Market Square is a 16th Century building.

Upper Stroud is by far the most attractive part of the town, a natural residential area above the busy town below. Walking through Stroud is quite rewarding; it is almost impossible to see anything by car because it is too busy with traffic, except on a Sunday.

Stroud, an industrial town, developed in mediaeval times, partly because it was blessed with ample water supplies from the River Frome and its tributaries, also because of the plentiful supply of wool from all around. At one time, early in the 19th Century, there were no fewer than a hundred and fifty mills scattered along the Frome and other streams. A few were for grinding corn but most were woollen mills, all powered by the flowing streams.

The Cotswolds were natural wool country in mediaeval times. Broad pastures on the uplands made ideal grazing for large numbers of sheep. The valleys all had streams, often swift-flowing, which never dried up and thus provided unlimited power. There were deposits of Fuller's Earth, an essential element in the processing of woollen cloth, and from both rivers and springs there was ample water for this industry, which requires such larger quantities for its many processes, apart from power to run the machinery.

Indisputable signs of wool processing have been found in many of the Roman villas which existed in such large numbers in the Cotswolds, traces of Fuller's Earth and so on. The Romans did their own weaving, at their villas, and are known to have exported heavy woollen cloths from the Cotswolds.

In mediaeval times carding, spinning and weaving were all done in homes, the fulling, finishing and dying processes being done in the mills. The Industrial Revolution with its machinery, soon put many of the Cotswold mills out of business and there was much emigration from the Stroud valleys. Yorkshire took over as the great wool county of England and the Cotswolds suffered. However, the mills which were able to survive carried on the great traditions of quality through all these difficult years, so that today, the Stroud region is still famous for broadcloths and others that are recognised as being the best in the world.

For some reason, this region has always specialised in broadcloths, so that Stroudwater scarlets and Uley blues became famous all over Europe for military uniforms. Today only six woollen mills are left but they still produce the highest quality cloths—again for uniforms and also for billiard cloth—which requires great skill and care. Collectively, they are known as West of England cloth.

In the days before railways, water transport was of vital importance to industry all over Britain. Stroud had to have easy access to bring in its raw materials and to export its finished products. The small rivers, even the Frome, were not navigable, so canals were dug. In 1779, the Stroudwater Canal was opened from Stroud down to the Severn at Framilode, making use of thirteen locks in its eight miles length. It was

An old lock on the Stroudwater Canal

still in operation until 1941. In 1798, the Thames-Severn Canal joined up with this one, coming down from Sapperton, on the Frome, at the head of the Golden Valley.

This canal was a remarkable piece of engineering for those days. It started near Lechlade, on the Thames, passed near to Cirencester after rising through sixteen locks, then five miles further on it entered the Sapperton Tunnel which was two and a half miles long. Barges were drawn along the canals by horses, but no tow path was possible through the tunnel. The barges were propelled along this two miles plus of total darkness by men lying on their backs on top of the boats and pushing with their feet against the roof. History does not say how long it took to get through to daylight again but it must have have been a long and arduous journey, with the difficulty of passing other barges coming in the opposite direction from time to time. In the Golden Valley, there were twenty eight more locks before this canal joined up with the Stroudwater Canal. By all accounts, these were extremely busy waterways, with a constant stream of barges passing both ways at all times.

The Golden Valley near Stroud

Parts of these canals are still visible, even in the middle of Stroud, now partly filled with bullrushes and other water plants. Further up the valley there are a few stretches with water still in them, and at Brimscombe I saw a family of swans swimming peacefully along a stretch of the canal. There was once a thriving port at Brimscombe but nothing remains of it today. Some of the brick-built, hump-backed bridges are still left—there are two or three near Brimscombe—and also several of the locks, though their wooden gates have long since disintegrated. Many parts of the canal have been filled in, others are filling up with natural debris, from plants and bushes and mud. Doubtless in time nothing will be left of them, a pity after so much energy was expended on their building centuries ago.

The tunnel still exists though, at Sapperton, but it has collapsed in places and would no longer be navigable even if there was water all the way through it. I was anxious to find the entrance at Sapperton, so I descended the steep hill from this most attractive little village to the Daneway Inn down in the valley.

I was told to follow the towpath for about six hundred yards, until I came to the tunnel. This I did, though the bank is very much overgrown and I was constantly ducking under branches and skirting round bushes on a very slippery, narrow little path. The canal alongside, was nearly filled in with small trees for much of the distance, but there were a few open stretches filled with water plants, a mass of lovely green. The entrance to the tunnel was quite undramatic, overhung with tall trees from the bank above, so that it was as dark as the interior of an old warehouse.

There are villages dotted all the way up the Golden Valley—first Thrupp, then Brimscombe, Chalford, Oakridge Lynch and finally Sapperton itself. Thrupp is notable for having an early 19th Century cast iron bridge over the canal, as well as two of the hump-backed bridges still standing. At Brimscombe, several of the old mills still exist, some in use though producing other things than woollen cloth today, and there are some good examples of the old mill owners' houses, usually above but close to the mills.

Chalford is built up on a particularly steep hill, on the north side of the river, almost a terraced town, with many streets too steep for motor cars. Again, many fine houses stand on the hill, built by the wealthy wool merchants. Between these fine mansions and the mills on the river below stand the weavers' cottages, often in clusters close to the mill they served. There are also mills on the south side of the river; one of the earliest of them all was built here. Chalford contains many relics of

Chalford, in the Golden Valley, near Stroud

the great days of wool in the 18th and 19th Centuries. Oakridge contains the last cloth mill on the Frome.

Sapperton, standing high above the valley, is a pretty little village, with an old Norman church named after St. Kenelm, one of the few. It is built on the hillside, with cottages at all different levels. The church was largely rebuilt in the time of Queen Anne, around 1730, the surprising point about it being the large amount of wood carving in the interior. This came about because, at the time of the rebuilding, Lord Bathurst was demolishing the old manor house, while he was constructing the great park and house at Cirencester, and some of the old Jacobean woodwork became available for the church. The carved pew ends are particularly good.

North of the Golden Valley there is a triangle of hilly country bounded on the east by Ermin Street, the Roman Road, and on the west by the Stroud to Painswick road. This is interesting country, laced with wandering country lanes, a land of often deep valleys, lofty hills, woodlands, some big estates and some particularly pleasant villages. It is totally unspoilt country, where little can have changed over many years, where the atmosphere seems to be eternally peaceful and placid. A tour of the various villages can be quite rewarding.

North of Chalford lies Bisley, a pleasant little clutch of Cotswold houses, with a tall-spired church standing out boldly. Like so many other churches, this one stands on the site of a former Norman edifice, and before that it seems there was a Saxon church. Its greatest treasure, however, is a highly decorated Norman font, on a modern pedestal, one of the finest examples anywhere of later Norman work. The church gained some fame from the fact that a hundred years ago its vicar was Thomas Keble, brother of John Keble. From 1862, he carried out considerable restoration work, strongly opposed by some of his parishioners, but largely paid for by himself and a few wealthy friends. In that year, two beautiful Roman altars were discovered and now rest in the British Museum. A Roman statue of Mars was unearthed in a field nearby.

13th century effigy, Bisley Church

Below the church, on the side of the road, are the Bisley Wells, generally known as the Seven Springs. Thomas Keble also restored these ancient springs, so that today five of them pour out from a curved wall, with another one on each side, a most unusual feature in this small village. On Ascension Day each year, the ceremony of well-dressing takes place here.

Close to the Bear Inn, an unusual building with outside columns supporting the upper floor, stands the village lock-up, a small building bearing the date 1824, with two small rooms heavily barred on the side facing the road. Next to the church is a fine mansion that once belonged to Elizabeth I, one of the many places where she is said to have stayed. A mile or so to the west is Lypiatt Park, where the Gun-powder Plot conspirators met to hatch their plot for the destruction of the Houses of Parliament.

A little to the east of Bisley lies Edgeworth, standing high above the upper Frome Valley. To reach the church, one walks or drives boldly through the manor house gates and along the drive. Just as the fine

The Severn Springs at Bisley

inner gates of the manor appear, with the elegant house beyond them, the church stands up a little on the left. It is all a most delightful scene, a perfect setting amidst noble trees for a manor house and associated church close by.

There are visible Saxon remains in the church, though some time long ago these were partly damaged when a heating system was installed. The south doorway is a beautiful specimen of Norman work, and the chancel is largely Norman, too. But the whole church suffered considerably by ill-conceived restoration work in the 19th Century. The manor house was built around 1700, on the site of a Roman villa, but has been added to at various times since. It stands in a commanding position on the hill side, with wide views from the far side.

A few miles further east still, in the little valley of the Dun, running down near to Cirencester, stand several delectable little villages of great beauty and interest. There is Duntisbourne Abbots, named not only from the river, as happens so often in the Cotswolds, but in this case from the fact that, many centuries ago, it belonged to the Abbey of Gloucester, being part of their far-flung lands. The church was Norman and contains some good Norman stonework, the font being a particularly good example of Norman work. The village is quite old and many of the houses are of considerable age. Long years ago, the stream was made to run alongside the main street so that farm wheels and horses' hooves could be washed easily.

Duntisbourne Leer, quite close by, belonged to the Abbey of Lire, in Normandy, hence the name. In 1416, it was given to the Abbey of Cirencester. There is no church here but several fine old farm houses, one with a large pigeon cote. Duntisbourne Rouse was named after the Rous family long ago. The church here was an early Norman one, but again it has been much mutilated during ensuing centuries. Parts of it seem likely to be Saxon and it is a church that will bear much careful exploration. This village is right on the river, the church standing above it on a steep slope, altogether a lovely situation.

Pinbury Park lies only two miles to the south-west, on the east bank of the Frome valley, one of the most superb of all the Cotswold Manors. It was the home of Sir Robert Atkyns, the famous historian, until his death in 1711. John Masefield, former poet laureate, lived there for some time. An Iron Age fort lies just to the north of the park.

Only a mile down river from Duntisbourne Rouse is Daglingworth with one of the most interesting of all the old Cotswold churches. This one was definitely Saxon, built on to by the Normans. But tragically, as is so often the case, someone thought it should be rebuilt and

A Saxon carving in Daglingworth Church

perhaps enlarged in the middle of the 19th Century. However, much of the original stone-work was re-employed, even the methods of use, so that there is much long and short work, typically Saxon, at various corners of the building. The porch was rebuilt earlier but almost all the stones are from the original Saxon church, possibly even from the doorway. There is a Saxon sun dial over the door, in very good condition.

During the 19th Century reconstruction, four carved stone panels of Saxon origin were discovered built in to the chancel arch, with the carving facing inwards. This had preserved them and they now occupy prominent positions in the church, perhaps the most interesting features of an old church that is indeed a treasure house of architectural material. There is even a carved Roman panel now built into the vestry wall, and a Norman altar, though not the main one. In the village there is a large dovecote, with over five hundred nesting places, and a revolving ladder to reach them, known as a "potence".

The Pigeon Cote at Daglingworth

Further north is Winstone, a straggling hill village of farms, with a Saxon-Norman church still containing many original features. The north doorway is Saxon, the south one Norman, and it seems likely that this church was built at the beginning of the Norman Conquest, employing both styles of architecture. There is little else of interest in the village but the church is well worth seeing.

A mile to the west, across the Frome Valley again, is Miserden, with a late Saxon church largely ruined by 19th Century restoration. But bits of Saxon work can still be seen, especially in the two doorways, and there are interesting Norman additions. The font at least is pure Norman and there are Norman windows, some blocked now. The church contains several good effigies on tombs. One stained glass window was presented by the Nizam of Hyderabad as a memorial to one of his servants, who was the son of the rector of that time. The 1914-1918 War Memorial is the work of Sir Edwin Lutyens.

The Golden Valley and the road (A-419) which runs eastwards to Cirencester, rather neatly divides the southern Cotswolds into two, though there is rather more territory to the south of the line than to the north. Between the Stroud valley and the Nailsworth valley just to the west, a narrow tongue of high land runs out, to drop abruptly down to Stroud below the point. This nearer part is Rodborough Common, and it merges into Minchinhampton Common, with no obvious dividing line. The whole is a more or less flat table-land of nearly a thousand acres, between the two valleys, with steep sides down into both of them, providing many excellent viewpoints and some splendid scenery. Most of it is now in the care of the National Trust.

On the west side of Rodborough Common stands a famous old hostelry, the Bear Hotel, now modernised, centrally heated and with some of the best food in the country. Expensive, yes, but a most comfortable centre from which to explore all this beautiful southern Cotswold country. It has been an inn continuously since it was built early in the 17th Century, though very much enlarged in the 1920's. Rodborough Fort, looking like a folly in the shape of a castle, stands at the point of land above the village of Rodborough. It was built originally in 1761 and stands out out boldly from below.

Minchinhampton Common, about six hundred acres in size, was given to the town by Dame Alice Hampton during the reign of Henry VIII. About the centre of it stands a signpost, marked Long Tom's post, where six roads meet. Highwaymen who were caught and executed on the common were buried at this spot. Not far away, on the

Minchinhampton side, a long bank stretches irregularly from one side to the other. It is known today as The Bulwarks, and is the remains of an Iron Age fort, believed to have been built some time before the Roman invasion of Britain in 43 A.D. This part of Minchinhampton Common is now a golf course, and a very popular one.

Minchinhampton was once an important cloth-making town, but today is a shopping centre and market town, quiet and peaceful, with a fine old Market Hall, built in 1698, and many typical Cotswold houses. The church is rather remarkable because of its strange tower. It looks as though it had once had a spire which was cut down and the edges castellated, and in fact this is just what happened, in the 16th Century. The church was originally Norman but has been very much rebuilt and enlarged at various times since those days, so that today it has a light and almost delicate appearance, undoubtedly one of the most beautiful interiors in the whole of the Cotswolds. There is a brass inside to James Bradley, the Astronomer Royal, 1762. In the churchyard there are some good examples of Baroque table tombs.

The Market Hall, Minchinhampton

Just south of Minchinhampton lies Gatcombe Park, a beautiful estate running down into the Nailsworth Valley. It was built in 1770 by a cloth merchant named Samuel Shepherd, later became the home of David Ricardo, the well-known political economist, and still later it came into the possession of Lord (Rab) Butler. It stands above Longford's Mill, with its large mill pond and ancient sluice gates on the dam, which was built early in the 19th Century. The first mill was built here in 1705, according to a date stone on it, and has been in continuous production ever since. At various times, it has been enlarged and modernised and today produces the high quality cloths for which this part of the Cotswolds is so famous. It is an ideal site for a mill, set deep in a wooded valley with its own lake, amidst the most beautiful scenery.

Two miles downstream in this valley lies Nailsworth, a busy little town on the river but now spreading steadily upwards on the steep slopes of the surrounding hills. Cloth is still produced here but Nails-

The Long Stone, Minchinhampton

The Mill Pond, Longford's Mill, Nailsworth

worth is gradually assuming the role of a pleasant residential area for the people of Stroud and neighbourhood. Upstream, beyond Longford's Mill again, we come to Avening, a pretty village in the wooded valley, with an old Norman church. At one time, the Samuel Shepherd of Gatcombe Manor was Lord of the Manor of Avening.

In the church there is a monument to Henry Brydges, a son of Lord Chandos. Brydges seems to have been a pretty lawless character, indulging in piracy and a number of highly doubtful escapades. But he redeemed himself by marrying Samuel Shepherd's daughter and settling down at Avening Court in the shadow of his prominent father-in-law, around 1600, to lead a later blameless life. There are several long barrows and tumuli close to Avening, including one with a large pillar of rock known as the Tingle Stone at one end of it. Close by is Norn's Tump, unearthed in 1809, which would appear to be as much as five thousand years old, an important historical find. Many Roman remains have been found all around Avening.

A few miles south of Avening, Tetbury stands at the crossing of six main roads. It is really just outside the hilly part of the Cotswolds but is definitely a Cotswold market town. Centred around a large 17th Century Market Hall, now the Town Hall, it is blessed with unusually wide streets. The name comes from Tetta, a Saxon abbess of Wimbourne, who founded a monastery here before the Norman Conquest. Again, this became a prosperous wool town and there are quite a few houses built by the more wealthy wool merchants. The church is mostly 18th Century, little of the original Norman building being visible anywhere. A number of monuments adorn the interior, with these words on one particular tablet:

"In a vault underneath
lie several of the Saunderses,
late of this parish; particulars
the Last Day will disclose."

Three miles south-west of Tetbury is Westonbirt, a public school for girls. In the five hundred acres of ground around the school is a famous arboretum, with trees from many parts of the world, open to the public and well worth seeing.

But now let us get back into the hills. Westwards, on road A-4135, is Beverstone, with the ruins of an old moated castle, built in the 13th Century, on the site of an even earlier one. It was besieged by the Parliamentarians in 1644 and eventually captured. The church is set among tall trees and was originally Norman, with quite a number of

100

Norman features left. There is a lovely piece of Saxon sculpture set into the tower but no other Saxon relics. The village itself is pure Cotswold, with stone-roofed houses and some fine old barns.

Newington Bagpath is as far again along the same road. It is set in a narrow little valley with fine views of the Cotswold hills all round, and a stream running through the village. It also possessed a castle in perhaps late Norman times, but all that remains of it today is a large mound, or motte, with a deep ditch around it. The church is quite plain but has a few remnants of Norman work, though much altered. Nothing Saxon is visible today, though it seems certain that this was a Saxon village a thousand years ago, named Bacwa. At the cross-roads nearby is a splendid big tithe barn, built about the year 1300, by the Abbot of Kingswood. More than a hundred and twenty feet long, it could hold nine hundred loads of corn and, though much altered, it is still in use today.

We are now at the head of a small valley running down through Lasborough Park to Boxwell and Ozleworth. Boxwell is hard to find because it is accessible by only the narrowest of country lanes. It is famous for a most unusual wood of box trees, covering a full forty acres. There is no village here, only Boxwell Court, a 15th Century manor house originally belonging to the Abbey of Gloucester, and the 13th Century church with an unusually large tower and some good features inside. It is recorded that Charles II sought refuge here after his flight from Worcester.

Ozleworth is another place where one goes boldly through the manor house gates and along the drive until one finds the church, passing the big house on the right, nestling very attractively among large trees, with plenty of space in front. The church is quite remarkable, having a hexagonal tower in the centre, all set in a circular churchyard, rather a rarity in itself. There was undoubtedly a Saxon church here, possibly the lower part of the tower even being situated in what was then a Druid burial ground. The Normans and others later added more to the tower, making it this most unusual church we see today. It is full of interesting detail covering many centuries.

Just to the west of Ozleworth is Newark Park, an extensive estate now in the care of the National Trust, with a large manor house dating back some centuries. The original house, it seems, was enlarged and restored soon after 1540, with stones taken from Kingswood Abbey, only a few miles away, when this was demolished at the time of the Dissolution of the Monasteries. It stands in a magnificent position, set

Ozleworth Church

in a beautiful park, and deserves to be better known.

We are now in the hills which form the southern part of the escarpment, with fine views from Newark Park and the slopes above Wotton-under-Edge. Wotton was originally a Saxon town named Wudetun, at the time of King Edmund of Wessex in 904 A.D. This most attractive little town is not as low down as the name suggests but is situated on a hill overlooking the valley. It is another wool town, and was very prosperous at the height of the wool weaving industry. It is said that Flemish weavers came and settled in the town in the 14th Century, so that probably for several hundred years, more people were employed in the wool manufacturing industry than in any other. Today, not a single wool mill remains, though there are a few in the neighbourhood.

There are some beautiful old buildings and groups of houses in Wotton today. The Tolsey, perhaps the most famous, was a court house and has a rather unusual pyramidal roof and cupola. An open space where a market used to be held is still known as The Chipping, from the Saxon word meaning a market. The Grammar School, one of the oldest schools in England, was founded in 1384 and produced a famous scholar by the name of Edward Jenner, the discoverer of vaccination. Isaac Pitman, the originator of short-hand, was a school-master at Wotton over a century ago.

Wotton church is a true wool church, light and airy with a magnificent tower, a most attractive building. No trace remains of any earlier church, believed due to the fact that King John's armies burnt Wotton to the ground, church and all, while fighting the Berkeleys, who were then powerful in this part of the country. The present church is 13th Century, much of the tower being Perpendicular in style, indeed, one of the finest examples of this type of architecture in the country. There are many monuments of various kinds in the church, some particularly good brasses and a fine marble tomb to Lord Berkeley and his wife Margaret, built in the early 15th Century.

The hills north of Wotton-under-Edge are very much broken up with small steep valleys, producing the most beautiful scenery and many a fine viewpoint. One road, B-4060, runs almost due north through North Nibley, along the edge of the hills and often part way up the slopes. It makes a big bend round Stinchcombe Hill to Dursley, a small town that is still very busy making woollen cloth and many other products.

Another road runs north-eastwards from Wotton steeply up on to the hills, and Dursley can be reached by making a sharp turn left on to A-4135. A left fork off this road leads up onto Stinchcombe Hill, instead of down into the town. There is a splendid golf course on Stinchcombe Hill today, and from the top, if you can avoid the flying golf balls, there are some of the finest views of all across the Severn Valley. Like so many of these escarpment hills, there is an old fortress on the top of Stinchcombe, probably Roman, though the ancient Britons may have had one much earlier.

Dursley is a busy town but has been little spoilt by its industry, largely engineering now. It has a fine pillared market hall, now the Town Hall as well, and a 14th Century church, much altered in later years. Again, a few of the old wool merchants' houses grace the town. Close by is the village of Cam, with a famous woollen mill still very

103

Wotton under Edge Church
104

much in operation.

Dursley is situated in a big bay of the escarpment hills, with a broad valley running up to Uley and two lofty hills left like islands in the valley—Cam Long Down and Downham Hill. Uley is a most attractive village, with an old church set high on the hill-side, with magnificent views, not only across the valley but up to the hills above, especially to Uley Bury Camp, the most remarkable Iron Age fort in the whole county. But more of that anon. There are some good table tombs in the church-yard, and some pleasant old houses scattered about the village. Uley is so keen to preserve its beauties that even bus shelters on the road-side are built of Cotswold stone, and become a natural part of the scene.

It seems that Uley was the first place in the Cotswolds where Spanish cloth was made. Early in the 17th Century, it is recorded that there

Downham Hill, near Uley

Box tombs in Uley churchyard

were some thirty weavers in and near the village, with another dozen or so at Owlpen, now a tiny hamlet a mile or so away. Owlpen is notable for the particularly fine manor house of mediaeval origin, one of the finest in the whole district. Above it stands an old church, both set at the foot of a lofty wooded hill. It is best seen from the winding lane that comes down into the valley from the Uley road above, a very narrow road, though it is also possible to walk in front of the building and to admire it from the broad steps running down from it.

A long hill runs up from Uley on the way to Nympsfield, with near the top a space for pulling in with a car. Here, after climbing a short hill track, one comes out on to the edge of Uley Bury Camp, with a double terrace where the original two ditches were built on the steep hillside, stretching far away into the distance. The camp covers a full

Owlpen Manor, near Uley

thirty-two acres, the whole flat top of it being a field, now ploughed and bearing crops. In its prime, hundreds of years before the Romans came to Britain, this great fort, with its ditches, steep banks and wooden stockade on the top, could probably shelter two or three thousand people of the local tribes, in time of danger. It has never been excavated and no one knows what treasures it might disclose.

It makes a splendid walk to go right round the camp on the higher of the two terraces. It is a mile and a quarter in length and practically level, working its way all round the sides of the great camp. The views are breath-taking on a clear day, in all directions. The two island hills—Cam Long Down and Downham Hill—stand out magnificently. Locally, Downham Hill is also known as Smallpox Hill; it seems that some long time ago, when there was an outbreak of smallpox, many of the victims were cared for in a hospital on the slopes of this hill. The

Uley from Uley Bury Fort

ruins of the hospital can be seen today.

A little further on from the entrance to the Camp, there is a sign-post on the roadside pointing to Uley Bury Tumulus. This is an excellent example of a long barrow, second only to Belas Knap, probably built at least four thousand years ago, with a properly constructed stone entrance, a central passage, and several small burial chambers inside. A number of skeletons were discovered in the chambers during excavations in the 19th Century. This burial mound has for long been popularly known as Hetty Pegler's Tump, from the name of the land-owner in the 17th Century. One can borrow a key to open the little door and go inside, from a local farm house. But it is a matter of crawling on hands and knees and with nothing much to see inside, except for the expert.

Entrance to Hetty Pegler's Tump, Uley

109

Carrying on along the same road, Nympsfield is a pretty little village with a square-towered church just off the road (B-4066) to the east. There is a gliding school here, as the hill formation is suitable for this form of sport and the village stands at over seven hundred feet above sea level. Another long barrow stands close to the road where we would turn off for Nympsfield. It is not in good condition and, indeed, after excavations many years ago, has been shamefully neglected.

The road (B-4066) back to Stroud runs right along the very edge of the escarpment, with Stanley Wood spreading down the slope. But the trees are so thick that, in summer time, almost nothing can be seen of the marvellous views. Only here and there is there the smallest gap which gives some indication of what one is missing. Here I would gladly see a few trees sacrificed, to give travellers a view they would not easily forget.

But instead of taking this road, we can go down a long, steep hill over the edge to Frocester, one of the Cotswold villages down on the plain below the hills. It stands astride cross roads, merely country lanes, well away from main road traffic. The manor house at Frocester is 16th Century, with a particularly beautiful gateway. This village also contains the largest tithe barn in England, being nearly two hundred feet long and thirty feet wide. It was built in the 13th Century and has apparently survived intact ever since then. It looks so absolutely right in these rural surroundings.

Little more than a mile to the east is Leonard Stanley, with King's Stanley merging into it. The former is named after the Priory of St. Stanley, founded early in the 12th Century by Roger de Berkeley. There are ruins of some of the buildings still standing, but the original church is virtually intact and is almost pure Norman, with a massive tower. The Priory lay immediately outside the church, the whole forming a compact group of buildings. In this village also, there is another tithe barn, not so large, but a very fine example and about the same age. The village contains several good buildings going back at least two or three hundred years.

The church at King's Stanley was also Norman, but remains of Norman work are now mostly confined to the tower. Again, there are some fine old houses, and a cloth mill five storeys high—Stanley Mill—erected at the beginning of the 19th Century. Built entirely of stone, brick and iron, even to the doors, window frames and beams, this was the first genuine fire-proof building in England. Machinery installed in this mill when it was built was still running in 1954.

110

Close to King's Stanley, the steep slopes of Selsley Hill rise into the sky. On the top is Woodchester, the site of one of the finest Roman villas ever unearthed in the country. Most of the treasures discovered are now in Gloucester Museum, but an extensive tessellated pavement, some twelve yards square, remains there. To save it from deterioration, it is covered with earth most of the time, but it is revealed to the public on special occasions.

And so we have now really explored the whole of the Cotswold escarpment, right from Meon Hill in the north, to the southern bulge by Wotton-under-Edge. It is a fascinating region of steep and often wooded hills, incredibly beautiful villages, small towns, manor houses and old churches, covering much of the history of England all the way from pre-Roman times, and we have seen some of the fairest scenery in all England.

CHAPTER VI

Following the River Coln

Let us go back to exploring more rivers now, and this time we will take the Coln, perhaps the choicest of all the Cotswold streams. It seems that there may be even more packed into its winding wooded course than that of the Windrush. But we will see, as we go along.

The Coln rises in a shallow valley between Cleeve Hill and the central hills of the Cotswold plateau, between Charlton Abbots and Brockhampton, flowing southwards past Sevenhampton and then ducking under the busy roads at the Andoversford junction. From then on, its course is through peaceful country indeed, a winding way past small cottages every mile or two, skirting big estates and passing through extensive woodlands, all the way down to Fairford which, like Witney on the Windrush, we will consider the last of the Cotswold towns on this river. It is only a few miles from here to the point where the Coln flows into the Thames, near Lechlade.

Charlton Abbots is a little hamlet with only a few scattered houses and a tiny church but with a magnificent Elizabethan manor house. The village is so small that it is easy to miss it altogether, especially as it lies off a quiet country road, the one from Winchcombe to Andoversford. But turn left and soon the lovely manor house presents itself, at a corner of the lane. Below it, the lane seems to go into a farmyard, but a footpath leads rather steeply down-hill, round a bend and there is the little church, on the edge of the fields, with a glorious view across the valley.

The church has only a bellcot, no tower, but the bell is believed to be six hundred years old. This was originally a 13th Century church but it was largely rebuilt around 1886. A pity, for little remains of the original Norman structure, except a door and a lovely old Norman font. At one time, Charlton Abbots belonged to the Abbey of Winchcombe and they ran a leper house here, though only the name lingers on today. Two Roman villas have been unearthed nearby.

Brockhampton is another small village just off to the left of the road. But its greatest glory is the Manor House, close beside our country lane, a beautiful building in a superb setting amidst noble trees, all part of a great deer park which lies on both sides of the road. The manor house is today the centre for research and development work of the Dowty engineering company, with factories in the Gloucester area. They keep it most beautifully, and it is a great credit to them. It is hard to imagine workshops and laboratories behind that beautiful Tudor facade.

Sevenhampton lies literally on the infant Coln, half of it on each side. The church is 13th Century and has some interesting old features, with a huge yew tree in the churchyard. The tower is central, resting on arches with internal flying buttresses in a most unusual way, with windows high up, shedding a lovely light below. This is, in a small way, a wool church, for a John Camber, whose brass is in the church, did much to improve the building before his death in 1497. A fine Jacobean manor house stands close to the church.

Brockhampton Manor

After escaping from the Andoversford roads and their noisy traffic, out infant River Coln meanders at peace for several miles as far as Withington. Here is a truly ancient site, for a Roman villa was found nearby; the Saxons built one of the earliest Cotswold monasteries here, about twelve hundred years ago, and then the Normans built a fine church in the village, much of which survives to this day, despite various restorations.

Across the hollow lane leading down into the village stands the Manor House, beautifully situated in a lovely garden, with the church tower clearly visible above the trees and a wonderful old pigeon cote in the grounds, in immaculate condition. What a collection of treasures! And down the lane, right on the river itself, the Mill Inn, creeper-covered and delightfully situated. It is not as old as it looks because it was, in fact, rebuilt as recently as 1960 but almost entirely of old stone, some of it from the former prison at Northleach. A good spot for refreshments, with chairs and tables in the garden beside the stream.

The Pigeon Cote at Withington

About three miles downstream lie the remains of Chedworth Villa, the best Roman villa to have been discovered in the whole country. Lord Eldon owned the land and was responsible for the excavations, between 1864 and 1868, for constructing the Museum and for building protective coverings over the mosaic pavements and bath houses, all at his own expense. It was a remarkable piece of work and we can see today most clearly how the wealthy Romans lived, how they heated their homes with a modern form of central heating, and we can gather how much they enjoyed their baths, steam baths, dry baths and large bathing pools. Theirs must have been a high degree of civilisation in many different ways. The villa became National Trust property in

Chedworth Roman Villa, mosaic pavement

Chedworth Roman Villa – the heating system

1924. Only half a mile away is the site of a Roman temple, from which many objects have been brought to the museum at the villa, but the site of the temple is overgrown, which seems a pity.

Chedworth village lies a couple of miles away from the river but is well worth seeing. It is quite a large village, spreading some distance along both the steep sides of a little tributary of the Coln. All the houses, and the church, seem to be on different levels, with the little stream splashing gaily about among them, hurrying always downwards towards the Coln. The church stands fairly high up and is Norman, with a good solid tower, Norman pillars and arches inside and many other survivals from Norman days. It is said that King Henry VII spent a lot of money improving this church, especially having large windows installed, and then seized the church and estates for himself. The pulpit is one of the best 15th Century carved stone pulpits to be found in the Cotswold churches.

Within a mile from the church there are two good long barrows, one thought to be at least four thousand years old, and in Withington Woods there are quite a number of round barrows, including one with an outer bank and ditch.

The small village of Yanworth lies on the hillside, well above the Coln on the opposite bank. There is little here but a few cottages and farm buildings, and the church. But this is a real find, one of the purest Norman churches for miles around. It is delightfully situated at the end of a little lane, set among old trees all by itself, so that perhaps for a long time no one ever thought of restoring it. Certainly there is much in this church that has remained just as it was when it was built, more than can be said of many others. The south doorway is particularly fine and looks as good as the day it was finished. The font is Norman and also the fine chancel arch, but there are, of course, parts which are later than Norman, including some of the windows. There are several scratch dials and a sun dial on the outside of the building.

Half a mile east is Stowell Park, a private estate with a large and magnificent manor house and a splendid little Norman church close by. The tower of the church long since collapsed and only the arches it rested upon are left. The greatest treasure here is some wall paintings executed about 1150 and still in remarkably good condition. They show seated figures which must be Apostles, and also a rather novel scene of Doomsday, with the rescued souls being lifted skywards by flying angels, and many figures below.

The Earl of Eldon, excavator of Chedworth Roman Villas, lived in the manor towards the end of the 19th Century and he had certain extensions carried out. Much earlier, it was the home of the Tame family, wealthy wool merchants in the 14th-15th Centuries, from Northleach. The house stands on a magnificent site above the Coln Valley, with superb views and an old water mill still operating down on the stream.

After flowing under Fosse Way at Fossebridge, with its pleasant country hotel, the Coln reaches St. Dennis and then a string of villages every mile or two down to Bibury. Each is a little gem in itself; we will look carefully at them all.

The Norman church at Coln St. Dennis stands in beautiful grounds, with wide lawns and a tiny stream running through them to join the Coln nearby. The church is almost as the Normans built it, most unusual. The arches and pillars of the central tower have sagged and bent somewhat during the eight hundred years they have been standing, and look rather curious both inside and out, though stable enough today. Beside the church, there are but a few pretty cottages, a 17th Century Manor House and the Rectory in the village. Its greatest charm is its utter peace and detachment from the busy world.

Coln St. Dennis Church

Coln Rogers was given to the Monastery of Gloucester in 1150 by a Norman knight named Roger of Gloster, but the church is much earlier. Indeed, it is the finest Saxon church in the whole county, with much long and short work, as well as Saxon pilasters inside. A lot of the original walling was built in Saxon times, and also the chancel arch. There are Norman additions, especially the south doorway and the font. Thus to this day, it is much as it was in Norman times, and like the church at Coln St. Dennis, has let the world go by and retained its peace and dignity. Only the tower is later, being Perpendicular in style. Again, there are but a few cottages and farm buildings here, not even a manor house.

Winson is barely a mile downstream, where the valley narrows quite appreciably, another small village of cottages and farm houses. The church is again Norman, an early one, which has been enlarged more recently, especially in the Middle Ages, when it was partly heightened. The font is Norman and the mediaeval porch protects a good Norman doorway. Winson Manor is an imposing early 18th Century house with much interesting interior decoration.

The River Coln at Coln Rogers

Ablington comes next, really a suburb of Bibury, and it has no church of its own. But it possesses a splendid late 16th Century Manor House, with two barns across the road, one enormous one that looks at first sight almost like a church. Another large building is Ablington House, an unspoilt 17th Century farm house, a truly Cotswold building. Over the door of the Manor House are five heads, of Mary I, Elizabeth I, Henry VIII, James I and Philip of Spain, with these words above:

"Plead thou my cause, Oh Lord, By John Coxwell Ano Domeney 1590" On the gateposts of Ablington House stand two stone lions from the Houses of Parliament.

Now we come to Bibury, one of the real treasures of all the Cotswolds. It has just about everything, a huge original Saxon church, a splendid Manor House, a famous hotel close beside the river, water

Bibury Manor

meadows filled with flowers in Spring and Summer as a foreground to a line of perfect Cotswold cottages known as Arlington Row. Near the hotel are trout ponds, where visitors watch the daily feeding, when the fish fight for the food and often push themselves right out of the water. And there is the old Arlington Mill, built in the 17th Century, probably on the site of a Saxon building long preceding it. In the 19th Century, the building was strengthened, and buttresses added outside, making it even more imposing.

In 1966 the whole mill was restored by David Verey, the writer of that incredibly detailed pair of books on Gloucestershire, one on the Cotswolds and the other on the Severn Vale and Forest of Dean area. Today it is a Museum and a most interesting one. In the 17th Century it was both a cloth mill and a corn mill at the same time. The village of Arlington, just up the hill from the mill, is a pretty collection of cottages round a green, with a Manor House. It is often missed by visitors who concentrate on the more immediate charms of Bibury itself.

Arlington Row, Bibury

Cotswold cottages at Arlington Row, Bibury, Gloucestershire

Coming down the valley from Ablington, we shall reach the Swan Hotel first, on the left, with its gardens beside the stream across our road. It is covered with creeper, tucked neatly under the steep hillside and is a famous old hostelry. Well named, there are almost always swans swimming in the river in front of it. The Coln is a good trout stream and fishing is available to the public. I watched a man one day casting superbly all down the stream, catching fish after fish, while a small crowd stood watching him on the footpath of a rather busy main road a few yards away.

This is the road running from Burford to Cirencester, and it seems a pity that it must run through Bibury instead of by-passing it. Just in front of the Swan Hotel, it takes a sharp bend over the river, on a stone bridge built about 1770 but still in use, even with today's traffic, though it is rather narrow. The mill stands a short way up this road on the right.

The Swan Hotel, Bibury

Arlington Row is a little further downstream, reached by an old footbridge and a pleasant path, with a small stream running in front of the cottages, beside the path. These were weavers' cottages, built early in the 17th Century, the weavers supplying cloth to the mill, after weaving it in their homes. Today the cottages belong to the National Trust, who act as landlords and who have done an excellent job of restoration over the years, and modernising the interiors.

The real village of Bibury lies at the far end from the Swan Hotel. In fact, if we had been coming in the opposite direction, we should have had the finest view of all, coming down the hill from Fairford, with Bibury Court across a sharp bend of the river, backed by wooded hills. Surely this is one of the finest manor houses anywhere, in one of the most beautiful situations imaginable. Almost at the same time, the tower of the church appears on our left and a road leads sharply down to it and to the collection of perfect Cotswold cottages clustered round the church gates. This is all quiet and peaceful, nicely off the busy road above, and here we can explore the church and its environs at leisure.

There is no doubt that this was one of the largest Saxon churches in the Cotswolds when the Normans arrived. In 1130 it became the property of the Abbey of Osney, near Oxford, and the monks of this abbey began an extensive rebuilding campaign. Hence we have to look rather closely for the Saxon remains, especially outside, though there is some particularly fine Saxon carving embedded in the north wall of the church. Inside, the chancel arch is supported on two very fine Saxon piers with some excellent carving on their capitals, and the string course is also Saxon. There are blocked windows which appear to be Saxon, but undoubtedly most of the church now is Norman.

Various styles in some of the details indicate that the rebuilding took place over some considerable time, even into the beginnings of Early English architecture. The font, however, is pure Norman, even to the pillars. There are some good brasses in the church and a number of typical box tombs in the churchyard.

Bibury Court turns out to be actually at a corner of the churchyard, though this is not obvious from the main road above. It was built early in the 17th Century by Sir Thomas Sackville, though an earlier manor house stood on the same site, so that Sackville may have really greatly enlarged the older building. Remains of a Roman villa have been unearthed in the woods of the manor house. Beside a farm-house near the church stands an old circular pigeon cote, with one gable and a turret on top.

Walking about in Bibury is most rewarding, for one can get away from the main road. A pleasant path threads its way from the old mill along the edge of the water meadows to Arlington Row and then on to the church and manor house, passing lovely stone-built cottages, often with flower-filled gardens. And every prospect pleases here in this scattered village. William Morris is credited with first noticing it and realising that it was something above average. He called it the most beautiful village in England, and this would, indeed, be hard to dispute.

King Charles II was said to be very fond of Bibury, mostly because in his time it was famous for horse-racing, having the oldest racing club in England. In 1681, the King was responsible for having the Newmarket Spring Meeting transferred to Bibury at the time when Parliament was meeting at Oxford. It was not clear where the race course was situated, possibly in the water meadows, but racing was certainly a popular sport at Bibury in the 17th Century.

Below Bibury there is a little clutch of three villages, all close together, three or four miles away. The first is Coln St. Aldwyns, reached by a country lane from near Bibury church. One of the beauties of exploring these Cotswold river valleys is that they are mostly served by country lanes, not main roads, so one can meander in peace, without being constantly "got at" by traffic or parking problems.

Coln St. Aldwyns is peace itself, with its Elizabethan Manor House and much restored Norman church. For more than fifty years, John Keble's father was vicar here, his son being his curate for his last ten years, until 1835. John, born in 1792, became famous for writing "The Christian Year", and died in 1866. They lived at Fairford, as there was not a good vicarage in the village in those days.

The Manor House was once the home of Sir Michael Hicks-Beach, Chancellor of the Exchequer, at the end of the 19th Century, who later became the first Lord Aldwyn. He rebuilt and enlarged the house, then a farm house, in 1896 and put his coat of arms over the front door. The manor farm barn is huge, with a date tablet on it marked 1700. Here again is one of the old pigeon cotes, this time a square one. Sir Michael is buried in the church-yard.

The village is built partly round a small green but climbs well up the hillside above an old mill on the river banks. One of the most attractive villages on the Coln, its cottages are typical Cotswold, with hardly a blemish in the whole lovely collection. The church stands at the top of the village with an imposing tower. Near to a blocked Norman arch, there is a curious piece of ancient sculpture of a demon attacking a man whose hand is firmly held in the demon's mouth. And there are other pieces of curious carving—some big gargoyles, a man blowing a horn and a fierce looking dog.

The porch is modern but it protects a particularly fine Norman doorway with richly carved capitals and zig-zag carving on the arch, in three rows, with dragons' heads on the hood mould. Inside, there is a beautiful stained glass window, erected in 1910 as a memorial to the Kebles, father and son.

All three of our villages lie on the edge of parkland, part of it Williamstrip Park, a large estate and deer park, with a great house built in the late 17th Century, it is thought by Henry Powle, at that time Speaker of the House of Commons. It has been altered on several occasions since, and was reduced in size as recently as 1946. It stands just to the north of the village of Hatherop.

Here, also, is another much larger house known as Hatherop Castle, a huge manor house, really, rather than a castle, an impressive jumble of gables, mullioned windows, chimneys and a tower with a turret. It is believed to have been built in the reign of Henry VII, though very much rebuilt at various times since then, especially in the middle of the 19th Century. The church nearby was also altered at the same time, though it was originally built not long after Norman times. There is a beautiful effigy in it of Barbara, Lady de Mauley, in marble, the work of Raffaelle Monti in 1848. Another, much earlier effigy, is that of a 14th Century priest.

Hatherop lies exactly opposite Coln St. Aldwyns, across the parklands, though it is Williamstrip Park which lies to the north, and the park surrounding Hatherop Castle to the south. The road runs between them, but it all looks like one. The village is a pretty one, just a small collection of somewhat scattered Cotswold cottages and houses, still with a feudal look about it, with an avenue of fine big trees running up to the castle.

Quenington is the third of our trio of villages, at the south-western corner of the parkland. Here, on the site of Quenington Court, the prsent Manor House, was the Preceptory of the Knights Hospitaller. The Gatehouse is undoubtedly Norman, as also is the circular dovecote, complete with potence, both probably from the early 13th Century. But that is all that remains of the original buildings. The present Manor House is 19th Century.

Quenington Church is dedicated to St. Swithin and is Norman, though substantially rebuilt in the late 19th Century, just another of the many tragedies perpetrated on the wonderful old churches of the Cotswolds. However, at Quenington, both the north and south Norman doorways survived, and they are among the finest examples in the whole region. The north doorway is protected by a modern timbered porch, and is richly carved with three rows of chevron patterns, as well as round mouldings. The capitals and pillars of the doorway are also carved with patterns of flowers and hearts, all the way down to the ground. The tympanum, the space between the tops of the capitals and the arch, has a marvellous carved scene showing the Harrowing of Hell, with Christ slaying the Devil with a cross, and three figures rising up beside Him, apparently from the mouth of a whale.

The south doorway is decorated with beak-heads, as at Windrush, as well as zig-zag patterns. Here also is a fine carved tympanum showing the Crowning of the Virgin, Christ crowning Mary, both of them

A house by the Coln at Quenington

sitting on a bench in a somewhat crowded scene, with buildings behind including a temple, though it is not possible to identify it with certainty. Inside the church, set into the walls of the nave, are various carved Norman stones, doubtless taken from the original church when it was "restored". It would be worth going a long way to see such wonderful Norman carved stonework as the two doors at Quenington.

Fairford lies only two miles or so to the south. We turn left along the main street, which is the road between Cirencester and Reading, rather too busy a road to go right through such a lovely old market town as Fairford. But the Market Place, the main square, fortunately lies just off this road, on the left. And what a perfect small town square it is,

127

The Market Square, Fairford

with rows of old stone houses, two old hotels—the Bull and the George—some fine big trees, and the church in the top left corner, with an early 17th Century school beside it. Beyond the church is the entrance to the beautiful park, though the great house, built soon after 1660, was demolished some twenty years ago.

The great church at Fairford, another of the wool churches, is famous first and foremost for its wonderful stained glass windows. The entire church, except for the base of the tower, was rebuilt at the end of the 15th Century by John Tame, a wealthy wool merchant, and finished by his son, Sir Edmund Tame, the Tames of Stowell Park. It is in late Perpendicular style, with no less than twenty-eight windows, all filled with glowing mediaeval coloured glass.

Nothing was too good for John Tame. He hired Barnard Flower, the

A stained glass window in Fairford Church

129

famous Flemish glass painter, who worked continuously in England for thirty years or so, from about 1495 to 1525. He became Master Glass Painter to Henry VII and was employed by the King to glaze the windows of the Lady Chapel in Westminster Abbey, and later the windows of King's College, Cambridge. He naturally brought over some craftsmen from the Low Countries, as they are today, but he also trained English glass workers in his methods.

Much freedom of expression was granted to craftsmen of every kind in those days, not only glass painters but wood and stone carvers. Hence we find in the Fairford glass windows Dutch scenes and buildings mixed with English subjects, even bits of Fairford church itself, scenes in the Coln Valley and the local flowers and plants.

John Tame's idea was to portray the story of the Bible, from Adam and Eve through all the Old Testament, to the life of Christ and finally the Day of Judgement. This last is portrayed in lurid detail in the three great west windows. There must be a thousand different figures in all this glowing glass, and untold details in the way of scenery and background.

One could spend many hours following the whole theme through from the Lady Chapel, where it starts. But inevitably it is the more spectacular parts which attract most attention, especially the great scene of the Day of Judgement. In a book called "A Cotswold Year", the author, a Mr. Warren, has much to say of this great scene:

"It is the devils which get all the attention from visitors. And no wonder. We all have a hankering after horrors . . . There is one blue devil, with white webbed feet, carrying off one of the damned in a bright yellow wheelbarrow, while a dark green devil prods the cart from behind with a red-hot poker. There is a blast furnace (or glassmaker's oven . . .) being blown up by two blue devils, and one can see the lost souls inside, impaled on forks, while the flames lick round them . . . But worst of all there is Satan himself, sitting with his hands upon his scaly knees, his long green tail winding about his feet."

And much more to the same effect. But Warren goes on:

"With such horrors to see, nobody bothers to look a second time at the procession of the elect winding slowly up the stairs to heaven. Hell is so much more exciting."

He explains that the 15th Century artists did their best with heaven, but:

"Their heaven is a pale and tame affair compared with hell, with its hosts of horned devils scuttling away with the damned thrown screaming across their shoulders."

But we should not be carried away like this; the stained glass of Fairford is far too beautiful and wonderful to dismiss most of it for the more spectacular objects. Every bit of it is worth a close look; it is full of unexpected treasures. It was saved from destruction by Cromwell's men by being buried in good time by the townsmen.

But John Tame provided far more than just these unique stained glass windows in his vast rebuilt church. He employed wood carvers of the highest skill to create screens on a scale rarely seen in any church today. Like the glass, they seem miraculously to have survived later fashions for the destruction of everything ornate in churches. There are oak screens, richly carved with patterns of fruit and flowers and leaves, running all round the chancel. The screen dividing the choir from the Lady Chapel has an arch in it which spans the tomb of John Tame. He lies there beside his wife, in effigy, with two angels guarding them. The choir stalls are also beautifully carved and the misericords are outstanding examples of mediaeval work.

Added to all this, there is some very fine stone carving in many parts of the church. Men with swords guard the corners of the great tower outside; there are rows of figures along the outside aisles, animals as well as humans; other animals hang from the window hoods. Most of the walls were covered with paintings, matching much earlier ones on the old part of the tower, though not much of this work survives today.

Fairford is a rewarding place to wander round. There are several very fine old houses, an old bridge that carries the main road across the Coln, and on London Road is Keble House, where John Keble was born in 1792. It will be remembered that he was the son of the vicar at Coln St. Aldwyns and became famous as the author of "The Christian Year." Some distance upstream from the main road bridge is an old mill, the mill house being 17th Century. Opposite the Park Farm is another old pigeon cote. Just to the west of the town lies an Anglo-Saxon cemetery, which was excavated in the middle of the last century, some hundred and thirty graves being discovered, with some interesting finds, now at Oxford.

So we have followed the River Coln all the way down its picturesque course, finding some of the greatest architectural treasures in all the Cotswold region and seeing some of the most beautiful scenery. We will leave the river here to wander its last few miles through meadows in flat country, to the point near Lechlade where it contributes its quite significant waters to swell those of the ever-growing Thames. Even London barges can get as far up the Thames as Lechlade.

CHAPTER VII

The River Churn

I have already described how the infant Thames, known first as the Churn, rises at Seven Springs, close to where the A-436 crosses the A-435 road. The first village it passes through is Coberley, barely a mile away. The church here is of special interest. It is reached through the archway of a farm, and we find the churchyard partly enclosed by a high wall, all that remains of the former Coberley Hall, a fine manor house which was demolished in the 18th Century.

The church was very much rebuilt around 1870 but was undoubtedly originally Norman. It contains several good monuments, the most interesting being that of Sir Thomas Berkeley, who fought at the Battle of Crecy, and his wife, with a small child close beside their tomb,

The Berkeley Tomb in Coberley Church

probably their daughter. Lady Berkeley was widowed in 1352 and later married Sir William Whittington. It was their son, Richard, born at Pauntley in 1359, who became the famous Dick Whittington, Lord Mayor of London three times over.

In the sanctuary of the church there is another effigy, a heart-burial monument and the only one of its kind in the Cotswolds, believed to be that of Sir Giles Berkeley, father of Sir Thomas. The heart, held in his hands, indicates that only his heart was buried here, his body being interred at Little Malvern in 1295.

It is believed that Richard Whittington lived at Coberley Hall for a time after his father, who became an outlaw, had died, leaving his widow to bring up the young boy. It seems probable that Charles I stayed in the house after the siege of Gloucester and that, unknown to anyone, his son spent a night here, disguised as a groom or servant, after the disaster of Worcester.

The village is quite small, with a rectory, a school and farm buildings. Two miles away is a good example of a Chambered Long Barrow, known as Shurdington Barrow, nearly 200 feet long, and another smaller one nearer to the church. On Crickley Hill, just over two miles from the village, there is an Iron Age Fort enclosing some six acres.

The next village, another mile downstream, is Cowley where the much restored Norman church has managed to retain a number of original features, including a very fine decorated font. The Manor House, built in 1674, was rebuilt and enlarged twice in the 19th Century, so that little remains of the original. The small river was diverted to make waterfalls and small lakes in the grounds.

Before we follow our stream further down, we should diverge for a couple of miles and go down the country lane running southwards from Cowley, over the hills to Elkstone, one of the highest of the Cotswold villages and one we must not miss on any account, for it contains one of the most perfect of all the small Norman churches. But the present one is decorated with various gargoyles, scratch dials, crosses and other carving, and was built about 1370.

A most unusual feature of the church is a pigeon cote above the chancel, with forty nesting places, reached by a corkscrew stairway from near the pulpit. There is a rich collection of Norman carving inside the church, with curious animals, signs of the Zodiac and quaint human figures. The chancel arch is magnificently decorated Norman, making this a truly remarkable church in so many different ways. Almost certainly there was a Saxon church on the same site before the Normans arrived. The original name of the village, according to the

Doomsday Book, was The Stone of Ealac.

Now back to the River Churn, and so to Colesbourne, with a huge park to the north of it, famous for its magnificent trees. Here Henry Elwes lived from 1854 onwards, a great lover of trees and co-author of a famous book "The Trees of Britain". He imported and planted all manner of trees from other parts of the world, in the park and the village, and there they stand to this day, a monument to his enterprise.

The hall is recent, mid-19th Century, and has largely been demolished and so is of little interest.

The church seems to have been Norman but has been restored far too much through the ages, though the south doorway and chancel arch are both 13th Century. The pulpit is the greatest treasure, one of the finest examples in the Cotswolds of 15th Century carved stonework, standing on a fluted column. One mile to the north is Norbury Iron Age Fort, while to the south a large Roman villa was unearthed just before the end of the 18th Century, with painted walls and mosaics still in good condition.

Our road downstream, the only main road which follows a Cotswold river for long, sticks close to the water and runs through some beautiful scenery, with woodlands and parks on both sides. On the left, high up on the hillside, we suddenly see a huge Italianate style house, entirely alien to the Cotswolds, yet quite magnificent in its splendid setting. It was built around 1860 by Sir F. H. Goldsmid, on the same site as two previous houses. Sir Edmund Tame owned this manor early in the 16th Century, the man who did so much good work, with his father, on Fairford Church. But his house was superseded by another one in the 17th Century, and finally by today's great building. Now it is a boys' school, Rendcomb College, founded by the Wills family in 1920 and quite a remarkable one. The idea was to educate "ploughmen's sons", for it was felt that, given the opportunity of a good education, working-class boys would shine in later life just as brightly as the sons of more wealthy men.

The church at Rendcomb was rebuilt by Sir Edmund Tame, as at Cirencester, and so it is not surprising to find some really notable woodwork in the form of screens, and some excellent glass, possibly some that was left over after the great windows at Cirencester were finished. The font is pure Norman, almost identical with the one in Hereford Cathedral. The wooden door is the original and has been in constant use since 1517. The three bells are mediaeval; the oldest was cast in 1450 and is one of the very few surviving Angelus bells.

The huge stables, across the lane from the church, are built round a

Norman font in Rendcomb Church

large courtyard, and are in themselves quite good architecture of their particular style. Today they are divided into various laboratories for the school, a useful arrangement, leaving the class-rooms and dormitories in the main hall.

North Cerney, two more miles downstream, is beautifully situated on both banks of the growing Churn. A grand avenue of trees leads to the old Norman church, one of the best in the Cotswolds. The south doorway is richly decorated in zig-zag patterns, five rows of them. It is believed that the door has been in use from about the year 1400, its decorated iron work still virtually perfect. It seems that a fire did much damage about the year 1470, and the church was largely rebuilt after that date. One delightful feature is a real rood loft, but this was built in recent years, most exquisitely done, as a war memorial after the first World War. The finely carved stone pulpit is a particularly good example of 15th Century work, and the font is also about the same age.

The old Church House was built about 1470, probably while the church was being rebuilt after the fire. The village itself is mostly of 17th and 18th Century cottages and houses. There is a Manor House at North Cerney, as well as Cerney House, itself a large house with extensive grounds and a long drive. Half a mile to the west is Scrubditch, probably part of Bagendon Dykes, a great Iron Age settlement with elaborate ditches and fortifications, and apparently something of a trading centre with countries on the Continent, even before the Romans invaded Britain.

Now we are close to Cirencester, the so-called capital of the Cotswolds, a town of outstanding importance in Roman times and a great market town right up to the present day. It is a lively old town of houses and guilds and hospitals from mediaeval times onwards, with some splendid old inns—the Fleece, Bear, Crown, Black Horse and King's Head—and a great market place right in the centre, dominated at one end by one of the largest and most magnificent parish churches in England. The history of the Romans here will be discussed in a later chapter; let us see what happened from the time the Romans came.

The church at Cirencester was built, or at least started, in the 12th Century, by Henry I. At the same time, from 1117 onwards, a great Augustinian Abbey was built close by. The abbot became the lord of the town, in effect, controlling virtually everything, jealous of his powers and immediately pouncing on any attempt at independence, or any industry which might compete with his. As Baddeley says:

"The Abbot blessed you, as rector of the parish church. Your grain

North Cerney on the River Churn

had to be ground at his mills on the Churn, and if you hanged, it was upon his gallows and at his orders."

But this is going ahead too rapidly. The Normans had built a castle at Cirencester, but during the Civil War with Matilda, King Stephen so wrecked and sacked the castle around 1140, that it was never rebuilt. Instead, the remains were used to complete the Abbey, in Henry II's time.

For nearly four hundred years the Abbey prospered and was a vital part of life for everybody within many miles of Cirencester. Then came the Dissolution of the Monasteries, in Henry VIII's time, and the buildings were sold to Roger Bassinge, on condition that not one stone be left upon another and that everything should be removed. Only the Hospital Gate, the old gateway into the Abbey remains, one of the interesting features of the town today. During excavations on the Abbey site in 1965, remains of a Saxon church were discovered, so this was a religious centre even before the Normans arrived.

All through the ensuing centuries, the great church was altered, added to, rebuilt and improved, to such an extent that it became one of the most splendid churches in all England, even including the cathedrals. The great tower was begun early in the 15th Century, and in this and the 16th Centuries, the wool merchants were responsible for many improvements and for some of the beautiful chapels built on to the body of the church.

Between 1515 and 1530, the nave was completely rebuilt. In 1490 the great South Porch was built, the most remarkable feature in the whole edifice. It is three storeys high, beautifully constructed and carved, with a magnificent fan vaulting ceiling on the ground floor. Some of the original doors into the church and the iron-work upon them, even the ring handles, are still in existence to this day.

This building was used for a variety of purposes, not merely as an entrance to the church. Financial matters between the State and the Abbey were settled here. It became a meeting place for Guilds and a variety of other purposes, even the Town Hall after the Dissolution. In 1831 it was decided that some of the many houses built on what is now the Market Place were too near, some almost touching it, in fact. So thirty of them were demolished. Today the Market Place is wide open of course, and one can see the great South Porch in all its glory from anywhere. During the last century, the entire porch was taken down, probably because it was thought to be unsafe. But it was faithfully rebuilt, stone by stone, exactly as it had been originally.

Restoration of the church has gone on more or less continuously ever since the wool merchants finished their beneficent work. Even Sir Gilbert Scott spent two years, 1865-67, doing a vast job of work, including replacing the old floors with tiles. The most magnificent view in the church is from the west end, down the whole length of the nave to the chancel, with the many high, almost delicate Late Perpendicular arches, the lovely screen and fine big windows at the far end.

There is evidence that, at the Reformation, all the forty two windows of the church, some of them enormous, were filled with mediaeval glass, as at Fairford. It does not appear to have been destroyed instantly, as in so many cases, but to have gradually disappeared over quite a long period. However, much of it was collected from various windows and re-set in just a few of them, so that today there is quite a good display of old glass in the church.

There are also many monuments and a fine collection of brasses. One of the best monuments is that of Humfry Bridges and his wife. He was one of the rich wool merchants who did a great deal for the church and the town. An unusual monument nearby is of the reclining figure of Sir Thomas Master, with open-necked garment and somewhat untidy appearance. A number of well preserved 15th Century brasses were brought together from various parts of the church by Sir Gilbert Scott and laid on the floor of the Trinity Chapel, a really fine collection. Other good brasses occur in various parts of the church. Many portray wool merchants and their families.

The pulpit is 15th Century, pre-Reformation, with beautiful open tracery stone carving, one of the best in the whole country. The ceiling of St. Catherine's Chapel has the most superb fan vaulting, the gift of the Abbot, John Hakebourne, in 1508. Although this was not the abbey church, the abbots regarded it with great esteem, hence such gifts as this one. The same chapel has some well preserved painted frescoes on the walls. An old effigy in the north wall is thought to be that of Richard Osmund, a purser of the Abbey well before the Dissolution.

One of the greatest treasures in this vast church is the Boleyn Cup. It is displayed in an illuminated recess in the south aisle, well protected by armoured glass and steel bars. It was made for Anne Boleyn two years before her execution, the cover having her personal badge on it. It was passed on to Queen Elizabeth I and she gave it to her physician, Dr Richard Master, who had acquired the lands of the Abbey after the Dissolution, and he presented it to the church.

Brasses in Cirencester Church

140

The great Park covers no less than three thousand acres and is open freely to the public by its owner, Lord Bathurst, though not for vehicles of any kind, not even bicycles.

It stretches for miles, with rides and walks and much good timber. The first Lord Bathurst, who lived to a ripe old age, was an expert on trees and, so to speak, designed his own park, with the most pleasing results. The Broad Ride stretches no less than five miles, in almost a straight line, to Sapperton, at the head of the Golden Valley above Stroud.

This was part of the great Abbey estates but came into the possession of the Bathurst family in 1690. Allen, the first Lord Bathurst, built the original Cirencester House early in the 18th Century, probably incorporating an earlier, Elizabethan mansion. It has been altered again since, but few people can see it today, for it is not open to the public but rests in the peaceful atmosphere of its beautiful grounds and lake. A thirty foot yew hedge partly hides it from view.

Perhaps after all this grandeur and antiquity, we have forgotten that we are following the winding course of the River Churn. It flows out from Cirencester through low meadows to enter the Thames near Cricklade, leaving the last of the Cotswold Hills around the ancient Roman city we have just been exploring.

But this is only one branch of the Thames, and a much disputed one. So we will go westwards from Cirencester and have a look at Thames Head, where the famous river is really supposed to rise. It is a disappointing search, for in summer-time, the spot called Thames Head, near the village of Coates and just north of Fosse Way, is completely dry. In a wet winter the meadow, known as Trewsmead, may become water-logged but this does not last long. We will probably not get our feet wet until we have walked two miles south, crossed the Roman road and gone some distance beyond.

The old canal which joined the Thames to the Severn, using the Sapperton Tunnel which we explored earlier, is nearby and now completely dry. Possibly building this so close to the original springs disturbed their source and drove them further underground. Anyway, despite the letters TH someone has carved on a tree near the spot, and the more recent erection of an old figure known as Father Thames from the Crystal Palace, it is an ignominuous beginning for such a famous river. When it does appear above ground, it flows only a few miles before it joins Swill Brook and then on to where the much larger Churn enters to make the beginnings of a real river. This is now outside

141

Cirencester town and park
142

the Cotswolds proper, so we will leave it to wander on its way to London and the sea.

CHAPTER VIII

Roman Roads in the Cotswolds

The Romans landed in Britain in 55 and 54 B.C. but did not stay. They returned after nearly a hundred years, in 43 A.D. and landed at Dover, Lympne and Thanet, unopposed. Meanwhile, between these two dates, Roman merchants had penetrated far into Britain, doing trade with a number of different tribes, and finding some of them bitterly opposed to others. So when the Romans finally invaded Britain, they knew a good deal about these many different tribes. Some were ready for protection against their local enemies and were willing to co-operte with the Romans. Others, under Caractacus and other leaders, bitterly opposed the invaders and had to be quelled. Gradually the Romans spread their power over much of Britain, pacifying the country by one means or another, bringing law and order and a degree of stability that was eventually highly appreciated by the native Britons.

Having conquered much of the known world already, the Romans knew only too well that the first priority was communications, and in particular roads. So they began to cover Britain with a network of their famous long straight roads, of which three ran through the Cotswolds. Fosse Way, perhaps the oldest, came down from the north-east, through what is now Moreton-in-Marsh, Stow-on-the-Wold, Northleach and Cirencester on to Bath. Ermin Street ran from Gloucester up Birdlip Hill, across the Cotswold hills to Swindon. Akeman Street went from Cirencester, across the Coln close to Coln St. Aldwyns, over the Windrush at Asthall and on to Bicester.

The first two are still main roads, long and straight, with few bends, but Akeman Street has long since disintegrated as a continuous road. It consists mostly of country lanes now but frequently disappears, though for many miles in places its course can be traced across the hills and the fields.

Buckle Street is often called a Roman road but it existed long before the Romans came, being an old British track which the Romans improved and used as one of their important roads. It came down from Bidford-on-Avon, to the north, arrived at the Cotswold escarpment near to Saintbury, climbed up there onto the top and ran along the edge of Broadway Hill to Bourton-on-the-Water, there joining Fosse Way. It is not as straight as others, but is a road with a purpose, nevertheless, with few divergences.

Besides these main roads, the Romans built many others of lesser importance, what might be called secondary roads, and also a number that were little more than tracks. Their greatest fear seems to have been ambushes, for each road was cleared of every tree, bush, house and possible hiding place, for as much as half a mile on either side. Curves were avoided wherever possible but there are many examples of Roman roads which are far from straight, often following hill contours. But in general the Romans always tried to build their roads in straight lines, at least from point to point.

These roads were well metalled, having a foundation of large stones, covered with rammed gravel, a surface that often had to be repaired. The width of their main roads varied from twenty-seven to twelve feet, and they were almost invariably made from local materials. Small quarries were to be found at frequent intervals along their highways, for both rock and gravel. Suppose we follow the three main Roman roads as they cross our chosen territory and examine the places they pass through.

Fosse Way enters Gloucestershire at Stretton-on-the-Foss, a few miles north-east of Moreton-in-Marsh. Today, Moreton is a pleasant little market town, having a wide main street with grassy verges, long rows of picturesque old houses and inns, and a Market Hall right in the middle of the street. The oldest building in the town appears to be the 16th Century Curfew Tower, at the corner of Oxford Street, a stone building with a bell dated 1633 which rang the curfew until 1860. The Market Hall is much more recent, being built in 1887.

The Roman road, and the more modern road on top of it until recent years, was originally two feet lower and was often flooded. But as there were no trees along the sides then, traffic was able to keep out of the water by running along the wide grassy verges, though doubtless not improving their appearance by doing so.

Stow-on-the-Wold, four miles on, is the meeting place for no less than five main roads, if we count Fosse Way, to the north and the south, as two. But miraculously today, none of these roads runs

Moreton in Marsh

through the town centre, which is an extensive irregular square with an old market cross, and a Victorian Town Hall, more or less in the centre, with a cluster of old shops around its walls. Near the east end is a huge elm tree with some lovely old Cotswold houses sheltering beneath its great branches, and of course not far away the town stocks. There are inns, and a hotel that was once a mansion, as well as shops and cottages, all conforming to the Cotswold style, a delightful but orderly mixture.

Stow is the highest town in the Cotswolds spurning the shelter of a valley like all the other towns, and is reputed to be a bleak and windy place at times. Perhaps that is why it was all built around the great market square, for the sake of shelter. It was a town of great fairs in days gone by, famous far and wide, when literally thousands of sheep would change hands. It received its royal charter to hold a market in 1107.

A corner of the Market Square at Stow on the Wold

Stow was a wool town, like so many others we have seen, and once more it was the wealthy wool merchants who enlarged and rebuilt the church during their period of prosperity, in the 15th and 16th Centuries. The 15th Century tower dominates the western end of the square, and the church is reached by a narrow street leading out from the north-west corner. The church was Norman, built on the site of a much earlier Saxon building, but every century up to the 17th is represented in the alterations and additions. There is much original Norman work to be seen, and quite a lot of Early English.

The last great battle of the Civil War was fought near to Stow, when Cromwell's forces thoroughly defeated the royalists, a thousand of whom were imprisoned in the church. This was in 1646, and soon afterwards it seems that the church was neglected and in very poor condition. However, restorations in the late 17th Century, and twice in the 19th Century, put it into the condition we see it today, a fine Cotswold wool church. Its greatest treasure is a large painting of the Crucifixion in the south aisle, a magnificent work of art by the Flemish painter Gaspard de Craeyer, a friend of Rubens and Van Dyck, and some think their equal. He lived from 1582-1669.

There is quite a good little museum in the Town Hall, with pre-historic flint instruments and arrow-heads, Roman tiles, pottery and coins, and some good relics from the Civil War. There is also a surprisingly good art gallery, with many paintings by Van Dyck and others, with portraits of Charles I, and of Elizabeth Bourchier, the woman of forty who married Oliver Cromwell, of Cromwell himself, Nell Gwynn and many others.

Stow is in the midst of beautiful hill country, with some fine woodlands and noble trees. Going south-westwards again on the Fosse Way, we run through dense beech woods on either side of the road on our way to the crossing of the A-40 Oxford road, close to Northleach. This town is not quite on Fosse Way but so near that it is the point from where we can explore it.

Northleach is truly an old wool town with one of the finest of all the wool churches in the Cotswolds. It was founded early in the 15th Century and prospered greatly in the 15th Century. The great church stands above the market place, its west tower a hundred feet high. Like so many of these churches rebuilt in the 15th Century, it is lofty and has a light and airy look about it inside, with much plain glass adding to the effect.

The south porch of Northleach church is one of the great ecclesias-

Northleach Church and village

tical glories of the Cotswolds, undoubtedly one of the most beautiful in England, with various statues and much good stone carving. The font is 15th Century, most elaborately carved, and the pulpit is also in carved stone, about the same age. In the church there are quite a number of good brasses, many of them to the wool merchants who were the church's benefactors. They are portrayed here with sheep, wool-packs, dogs, and other animals and one, a tailor, even with a pair of scissors.

The town, busy though it was in mediaeval times, has been content to relax since then, so that today it seems more like a large village going quietly about its business with no fuss and bother, letting the busy world go by on its hectic missions, without affecting it. It seems a pity that the busy Oxford road has to go right through the town instead of round it somewhere.

Now we can carry on south-westwards along Fosse Way to Cirencester, crossing the Coln on the way to Fossebridge. We have already seen what Cirencester is like today; now we will try to describe what it must have been like in Roman times.

The Romans swept across the Cotswolds during their first few years in Britain, making a fort at Glevum (Gloucester) and using the Severn as a defence line, by the year 49 A.D. They also built the Fosse Way as a vital line of communication, to move troops quickly and to ensure supplies reaching their forward areas. Corinium (Cirencester) was an important junction of five roads, so very soon a fort was built here, improved and rebuilt more than once in the next half century. A civilian settlement arose outside the fort and by 60 A.D. many of the local Dobunnic tribes people began to move into it, doubtless feeling more secure there. Soon this became the tribal administrative centre for the Dobunni, hence its full name, Corinium Dobunnorum.

As the Romans advanced further into Wales and Northern England, these two fortresses became less important and were finally evacuated by troops in the later part of the 1st Century. Glevum declined in importance but Corinium grew considerably as a civilian centre for many years, so that by the end of the 2nd Century the great defence walls, said to be ten feet thick and thirty feet high, enclosed nearly two hundred and fifty acres. A large forum was built and also a basilica which, as a result of recent excavations, is now known to have been nearly three hundred feet in length. Corinium, in fact, became the second largest Roman city in England, having a population of five thousand people, exceeded only by Londinium (London).

It was, in fact, a larger town than it is today, a walled and moated city, with its own local Senate, law courts and electors. The Romans also built a grammar school where the local people were educated—in the Latin language!

There were many wealthy houses in the town and a number of large Roman villas in the neighbourhood, some of which have been excavated in recent times. Others will doubtless be found. This must have been a wealthy region but it is not clear how the wealth arose or what the main industries were. When the Romans departed, late in the 5th Century, Corinium remained prosperous and orderly for a long time, but gradually declined until it was taken by the invading Saxons.

The Roman walls remained standing, though slowly decaying, certainly until the 15th Century. Leland, that great recorder of history in the time of Henry VIII, describes one tower still standing in 1540. Doubtless these great walls formed a convenient and handy quarry for the local people, and if we knew where to look, we should find many of the stones in the walls of surviving mediaeval houses in present-day Cirencester.

Remains of the Amphitheatre, now known as the Querns, or Bull Ring, are still clearly visible today outside the town, with grassy banks nearly thirty feet high. The arena measured a hundred and sixty feet long and over a hundred and thirty feet wide, surrounded by terraces of seats, with long entrance passages. It can be reached by a footpath just west of the railway bridge. Smaller remains of the basilica can be seen in the town, near Tower Street.

Fosse Way now pursues its way south-westwards towards Bath along the southern edge of the Cotswold Hills, and so we will leave it here and trace the other Roman roads.

Ermin Street starts from Gloucester and climbs the Cotswold escarpment by the prodigious Birdlip Hill. No hair-pin bends for the Romans, no diagonal roads across hill slopes, if there was a direct way up. Steepness did not matter; more horses could be used. And this applied for many hundreds of years after Roman times.

The art of road-making declined sadly after the fall of the Roman Empire. Our roads in Britain became uncared for tracks, with no concerted programme of maintenance worthy of the name. It was Telford and MacAdam, at the end of the 18th Century, who really began to rebuild our roads, Telford with his astonishing engineering capacity, MacAdam with his invention of the macadam road surface, named after him and long after his death improved by the use of tar to make hard-surfaced roads in the motor age.

In the centuries during which road surfaces declined in Britain, one of the greatest problems with coaches and other vehicles was mud during wet weather, and soft boggy surfaces due to too much water. Hills were actually preferred to level surfaces because they were naturally drained, by gravity. So many a road took to the hills, and the shortest way up the hills, and often the steepest, partly to avoid unnecessary miles and partly because the surface would be better than on level ground. Heavier coaches and more horses overcame the problems, whereas the real answer was improved and harder surfaces. It took thirteen centuries after the Romans left for the people of Britain to learn this fundamental truth, and it was MacAdam who taught them. The Romans had learnt it early in the Christian era, or even before it dawned, and they had the sense to maintain their roads properly and continuously.

Therefore Birdlip Hill is no surprise. There are other steep Roman roads in different parts of the country, especially in Wales and in the Lake District, so Birdlip is no exception. The surprising thing is, perhaps, that in our own day we have not made a new road up to the escarpment, with many bends and twists to cut down the gradient. But we have not, and the present A-417 seems to be built exactly on the site of the original Roman road.

Tiles and other Roman remains have been found all round the Royal George Inn at the top of Birdlip Hill, for it seems that the Roman staging post here was on exactly the same site. The road then runs nearly straight along the tops of the hills, through beautiful woods today, not cut back from the road at all as they would have been in Roman times, all the way to Cirencester, and far beyond in the same direction. There are no villages actually on this stretch of road.

Akeman Street starts at Cirencester and runs in a pretty straight line all the way to Bicester. Here it turns somewhat south and aims straight for London, along what is now A-41. It passes through no towns or villages during its passage through the Cotswolds, not even the parts which have now disappeared. But it was an important road in Roman times and one which helped to make Cirencester such a prominent town.

Buckle Street is a country road all the way from Bourton-on-the-Water to Saintbury, where its true line seems to get lost. However, from the foot of the escarpment nearby it can be picked up again, running more or less straight northwards, and here sometimes known as Icknield, or Ryknild Street, a true Roman road which went right through the Cotswolds southwards in a most direct way, somewhat to the east of the not-so-straight Buckle Street. Ryknild Street has almost entirely disappeared today in the Cotswolds and is at best only a country lane here and there.

CHAPTER IX

Following the Evenlode

The River Evenlode runs down the eastern part of the Cotswold plateau, really just beyond it, where the Cotswolds enter Oxfordshire. Strictly speaking, we need not include this stream and its villages in the Cotswolds, as we have really confined our subject to the main, unbroken block of hills, mostly in Gloucestershire. But somehow our story would not be complete without at least glancing at this river with its lovely name, and the valley through which it flows.

The Evenlode rises in the hills near to Moreton-in-Marsh, with several tiny tributaries coming down into the valley to make a visible stream a couple of miles south of the town. Then it wanders, with many a twist and turn, through a broad green valley of fields and farms and many fine trees, southwards and a little east as far as the three Wychwood villages. It is not a typical Cotswold valley, for the hills are missing, as well as the stone walls and the beech woods. Evenlode village, too, is not quite genuine Cotswold, for it has a few slate roofs instead of the familiar thin stone slabs. But it has some excellent Elizabethan buildings—Evenlode House—right in the village, and some fine old Elizabethan farm houses nearby.

The church is very much like a number of those we have seen in the hills, with a late Norman chancel arch. A particularly splendid carved oak pulpit and a fine heraldic font are both some five hundred years old, and here also is something very unusual—a sanctuary chair, carved in stone. Only about four of them are to be found now in the whole country. They existed for a peculiar purpose. When a man had committed some serious crime and was likely to be apprehended, he could make for the church and seat himself in the sanctuary chair, where the law could not touch him. But he had to admit his crime officially, and then leave the country within a very short time, perhaps only a few days, and never return to his homeland again.

The Evenlode villages have produced some famous people in their time. Warren Hastings, first Governor-General of India in 1773, lived at Daylesford as a boy and also in the later part of his life. The village and surrounding land had belonged to the Hastings family since the 12th Century but had been lost in the Civil War because the Hastings were royalists. Warren's ambition, even as a poor boy, was to own it all again, but this took a long time. He was absent for more than thirty years but during that time, he acquired both fame and fortune in India, though he returned to England to face impeachment on charges of corruption and excessive cruelty.

The trial was to take seven years, from 1788 to 1795, but nothing daunted, Warren returned to Daylesford soon after his return from India and, miraculously, the estate came on to the market and he was able to buy it. Even during the long period of the trial he rebuilt the manor house, the present Daylesford House, and thus in fact became the local squire. But the trial cost him all his remaining fortune, and it was only due to the generosity of the East India Company, who gave him a substantial pension, that he was able to live the life he yearned for over such a long period. He died in 1818 and is buried in the local church.

Kingham, just over the border of Oxfordshire, has a 14th Century church with unique pews. They are all made of stone, beautifully carved, only the seats being of wood. Cold, no doubt, but most impressive, unlike anything we have ever seen in the Cotswolds.

Kingham was the home of William Warde Fowler, the great bird lover, an Oxford don, who wrote many books which are now regarded as classics, one of them being "Kingdom Old and New." He died in 1921 and there is a brass to him in the church.

Another famous Kingham man was Charles Baring Young, a wealthy aristocrat who founded a secret charity for poor city boys. Even as a boy at Eton, he began to feel that something should be done for under-privileged boys, and in his youth he took a party of slum boys with him on his holidays. Later, he used three large houses in Fitzroy Square in London, to house sixty-six homeless boys, before moving back to his estate at Daylesford.

Once home again, he built eight large houses near Kingham, known as the Kingham Homes, housing thirty boys in each, with work-shops, instructors and class-rooms. Then he founded two factories and ran a five hundred acre farm, to give employment to some of the boys, under expert tuition.

He also bought a lot of land in Canada, so that any boys who wished to emigrate could go and set up home there. And all this time he shunned every form of publicity and his family and friends were sworn to secrecy. Finally, he endowed all his homes so substantially that they never had to seek funds outside.

A couple of miles or so south-west of Kingham lies Idbury, formerly the home of Sir Benjamin Baker, a famous engineer who built the first tube railway in London, the Central Line, and was also the designer of the Forth Bridge and the Assuan Dam in Upper Egypt. He was born in 1840 and died in 1907. Here also, in this remote spot, was born that famous quarterly "The Countryman", now produced at Burford, as we have already seen.

Idbury is a real hill village, bleak at times, with wide views across the countryside and down into the Evenlode Valley. Its church is Norman and there is a Tudor manor house. Much 13th Century work is to be found in the church but nothing of great importance later. There is a splendid doorway and the rood stairs are still there. The font is more than six centuries old.

At Shipton-under-Wychwood, the Evenlode takes a big bend to the north-east and the hills approach a little closer. Shipton Court is a magnificent Elizabethan Manor House, suddenly coming into view when one has walked or driven along by a high wall to an opening and a big gateway, with the most enchanting view of this great house, well set back in a perfect setting. The steeple of a 13th Century church shows above the trees nearby. It is rich with stone carving, much of it from 15th Century rebuilding. William Langland lived here, famous for his 14th Century poem "Piers Plowman". He was probably educated at Malvern Monastery.

Ascot-under-Wychwood lies a mile or so downstream, with a manor house and a Norman church that is, miraculously, still mostly Norman, with a lovely doorway, massive pillars and a Norman window. Wychwood Forest, however, what is left of it, lies further downstream, though doubtless it once covered all the hills to the south of the Wychwood villages.

Soon after the river turns south-eastwards again, we come to Charlbury, and here is a true Cotswold village, with a delightful main street running down-hill towards the square-towered church, with a string of genuine stone houses, old inns and cottages, many gay with flowers, along each side. The church is a mixture, with some original Norman work to be seen, more 13th Century and later, with a painted sun dial on the outside, over two hundred years old. Dr Ralph Hutchinson, to whom a tablet was erected near to the pulpit, was vicar here from 1593 to 1606. He was the President of St. John's College, Oxford, and a translator of the authorised version of the English bible.

At the vicarage, Anne Downer was born. She married a Quaker in 1624 and was the first woman to preach in public in London. Her husband was persecuted and died at Newgate. She later married George Whitehead, the famous Quaker, and worked with him for a long time. So it is not surprising that there is a nice little Friends Meeting House still to be found in Charlbury.

Just across the river from the village lies Cornbury Park, with its huge Manor House, the largest house in Oxfordshire until the building of Blenheim Palace. Originally 15th Century, it was rebuilt in the 17th. Robert Dudley, Earl of Leicester in Queen Elizabeth's time, lived here and died in the great house. Charles II was royally entertained there, on at least one occasion. It is said that later on there was Jacobite intrigue and plotting at Cornbury House, and even that Charles Edward himself was sheltered here, and also discovered, by a barber.

Beyond Charlbury, the Evenlode winds and twists mightily, running alongside Woodstock Park for a short way, and past the village of Bladon, where Sir Winston Churchill lies in the churchyard, and so into the Thames a few miles above Oxford. But this is not our Cotswold country, so we will leave this sparkling little river to join the larger one and make its way to the sea.

We cannot, however, leave the Cotswolds without looking at a truly Cotswold market town, though it is somewhat to the east of the main block of hills. It is Chipping Norton, only a few miles north-west of Charlbury; and on a tributary of the Evenlode. It is a real hill-top town, with a main street so wide that it is also a market place, and a very important one for many centuries. Chipping Norton was a busy wool town and tweeds are still made there, at a famous mill down in the valley. Two large buildings stand out in the centre, one the Town Hall, the other the Old Guildhall, at either end of the Market-place.

Here again is a beautiful wool church, as might be expected, mostly 14th and 15th Centuries, though on an earlier foundation. It is surprisingly light and airy, with tall slender columns and many windows, some with outstandingly good glass. There are some good tombs in the church and a number of excellent brasses, mostly 15th Century, again with wool packs and sheep quite prominent. Outside the church are some grassy mounds, all that remains of an ancient castle from Norman times.

Three miles north of Chipping Norton stands one of the most famous ancient monuments in the country—the Rollright Stones. They consist of a stone circle, a group of larger stones known as the Whispering Knights, at the side of a country lane, and the single King Stone on either side. This was evidently an important road long before the Romans ever came to Britain and the stones were in a prominent position.

The five Whispering Knights are the remains of megalithic structures underneath a long barrow which has disappeared untold ages ago. The Stone Circle is some hundred feet across and both this and the long barrow must have been built at least 2,000 years before Christ, before the dawn of Druidism. Professor Alex Thom maintains, with much conviction, that this and many other groups of ancient stones all over Britain are collectively part of a system of highly developed observatories. Sir Arthur Evans, famous for his work at Knossos, on Crete, visited the Rollright Stones in 1890 and was so impressed that he wrote a paper on the old folk stories which have accumulated about them, all about witches, fairies and supernatural events. These ancient stones are now in the care of the Department of the Environment.

And so we have explored the Cotswolds from end to end, from north to south and from east to west. We have seen a lot of the beautiful scenery, many of the stone-built villages and small towns, we have gone into the little country churches and the great wool churches of the towns that thrived on wool for centuries in mediaeval times—and we have followed the rivers through their green valleys. We have discovered ancient burial mounds thousands of years old, and climbed up to Iron Age forts on hill-tops overlooking the vast plain of Gloucestershire and the broad valley of the Severn, far away to the Welsh mountains. And all through these wanderings we have delved into the history of the region, right from the Stone Age people who once lived here, through the Roman, Saxon and Norman invasions to more recent times. We have not seen everything, not walked through every village or seen every manor house and church. But we have seen enough, I think, to make us realise that this is, indeed, a part of Britain that is immensely rich in so many different ways.

Ablington, 120, 122
Andoversford 74, 112
Anne, Queen 45
Ashton-under-Hill 12
Asthall 41, 144
Asthall Leigh 43
Aston-sub-Edge 12, 52
Atkyns, Sir Robert 93
Avening 100

Baker, Sir Benjamin 156
Barrington, Great & Little 31, 33
Bathurst, Lord 141
Berkeley family 103, 132, 133
Beverstone 100, 101
Bibury 118, 120, 121, 123, 124, 125
Birdlip 12, 74, 75, 144, 151, 152
Bishop's Cleeve 12
Bisley 91, 92
Bladon 158
Boleyn, Anne 78, 83, 139
Boteler, Ralph 67, 69
Bourton-on-the-Water 24, 25, 26, 145, 152
Boxwell 101
Bradley, James 97
Bray family 31
Bredon Hill 12, 58
Bredons Norton 12
Brimscombe 89
Broadway 12, 46, 52, 53, 55, 58, 74, 145
Brockhampton 70, 112, 113
Bryan, John 82
Brydges, Henry 100
Buckland 12, 64
Burford 35, 36, 38, 39, 40, 41, 122, 156
Burne-Jones 58
Butler, Lord 98

Cam 103
Cam Long Down 105, 107
Chalford 89, 90, 91
Charlbury 156
Charles I 55, 82, 83, 133
Charles II 101, 124, 157
Charlton Abbots 112
Charlton Kings 71, 74
Chandos family 67
Chedworth 117
Cheltenham 12, 55, 66, 70, 71, 73, 74, 84
Chipping Campden 12, 48, 50, 51, 52
Chipping Norton 158
Churn – River 13, 74, 132-143
Cirencester 15, 74, 75, 87, 90, 93, 96, 122,
    136, 138, 139, 141, 144, 149, 150, 151, 152

Clapton 30, 31
Cleeve Hill 12, 66, 69, 70, 71, 112
Coates 141
Coberley 132
Coke, Sir Edward 43
Colesbourne 134
Coln – River 13, 112-131, 144
Coln Rogers 119
Coln St. Aldwyns 125, 144
Coln St. Dennis 118
Conderton 12
Cooper's Hill 12
Coventry, Earl of 58
Cowley 133
Craik, Mrs. 73
Cranham 74
Cricklade 13, 141
Crickley Hill 12
Daglingworth 93, 95
Daylesford 159
Dent family 67
Dikler – River 26, 29, 31
Dover's Hill 52, 53
Dover, Robert 52
Dover, Thomas 61
Downer, Anne 157
Downham Hill 105, 107
Dudley, Robert 157
Dumbleton 12
Duntisbourne Abbots 93
Duntisbourne Leer 93
Dursley 103, 105
Dutton, Thomas 35

Ebrington 51
Edgeworth 92, 93
Edward I 39
Edward III 39
Edward VI 67
Edwardes, Thomas Dyer 78, 79
Eldon, Lord 115, 117
Elizabeth I 40, 69, 92, 120, 139
Elizabeth II 45
Elkstone 133
Elmley Castle 12
Elwes 133
Evenlode 153
Evenlode – River 13, 153-158
Evesham 46, 58
Eye – River 26, 28

Fairford 112, 127, 128, 130, 131
Farmington 34, 35
Faulkner family 40

Fettiplace family 41
Fish Hill 53
Flower, Barnard 128, 130
Ford 18, 61
Fossebridge 118
Fosse Way 15, 24, 25, 35, 118
Fowler, William Warde 155
Frocester, 110
Frome – River 86, 90

George III 71
Giffard family 75
Gloucester 15, 84
Grafton 12
Great Comberton 12
Grevel, William 50
Guiting Power 18, 20

Hampton, Dame Alice 96
Haresfield Beacon 84
Hastings, Warren 155
Hatherop 125, 126
Henry I 136
Henry III 64, 65
Henry VII 117, 130
Henry VIII 59, 65, 66, 78, 83, 120
Hicks, Sir Baptist 48, 50, 51
Hicks-Beach, Sir Michael 125
Hidcote 12, 13, 46, 51, 52
Hill, Len 26
Hinsley, Cardinal 79
Holst, Gustav 31, 73
Howard, F. E. 24
Hutchinson, Dr Ralph 156

Idbury 156
Ilmington Down 51

Jackson, Sir Thomas 25
James I 40, 120
Jenner, Edward 103
John, King 39
Johnstone, Laurence 51
Keble, John 125, 131
Keble, Thomas 91
Kennedy, Margaret 73
Kineton 18
Kingham 155
King's Stanley 110, 111
Kingston, Sir Anthony 83

Lacey, Gilbert de 18
Langland, William 156
Langley Hill 67, 69

Latimer, William 53
Lechlade 112, 131
Leckhampton Hill 12, 74
Lee, Philip 34
Lenthall – (Speaker) 39, 41
Lovell family 43, 44
Lutyens, Sir Edward 29, 96

Malvern Hills 58
Mary I 120
Masefield, John 93
Master, Dr Richard 139
Meon Hill 12, 13, 46, 51, 52
Mickleton 52
Minchinhampton 96, 97, 98
Minster Lovell 43, 44
Miserden 96
Mitford, Nancy 41
Mitford, Unity 41
Monti, Raffaelle 126
Moreton-in-Marsh 144, 145, 153
Morris, William 58, 124

Nailsworth 98, 100
Naunton 11, 20, 22, 23, 24
Newington Bagpath 101
Norbury Camp 35
North Cerney 136
Northleach 144, 148, 149
North Nibley 103
Nottingham Hill 12, 69
Nympsfield 106

Oakridge Lynch 89, 90
Oldys, Ambrose 22
Oldys, Dr William 22
Overbury 12
Owlpen 106
Oxenton Hill 12
Ozleworth 101

Painswick 74, 80, 82, 83, 84
Parr, Catherine 67
Phillips, Sir Thomas 55, 58
Philip of Spain 120
Pitman, Isaac 103
Powle, Henry 125
Prinknash 74, 78, 79, 80

Quenington, 126, 127

Redesdale family 41
Rendcomb 134
Ricardo, David 98

Richard II 39
Richard, Earl of Warwick 39
Rissingtons – Great & Little 30, 31
Robinson brothers 58
Rodborough 96
Rosetti 58

Saintbury 53, 58, 145, 152
Salmonsbury 26
Salperton 34
Salter's Hill 66
Sapperton 88, 89, 90, 141
Scott, Peter 26
Scott, Sir Gilbert 67, 139
Scott, Sir Walter 73
Selsey Hill 111
Sevenhampton 112, 113
Severn – River 11, 15, 47, 84, 86
Seymour, Lord Admiral 67
Shab Hill 12
Sherborne 35
Sherborne family 35
Shipton-under-Wychwood 156
Shortwood Hill 84
Slaughter, Upper & Lower 26, 28, 29
Snowshill 55, 58, 61
South Hill 12
Stanton 12, 61, 64
Stanway 12, 18, 61
Stinchcombe Hill 103
Stott, Sir Philip 64
Stow-on-the-Wold 144, 145, 146, 148
Stratford-on-Avon 74
Strong, Thomas 34
Strong, Valentine 34
Stroud 12, 13, 46, 74, 84, 85, 86, 88, 89, 96,
    100
Sudeley 66, 67
Swells, Upper & Lower 26
Swinbrook 41, 43
Talbot, Lord 31, 33
Tame family 118, 128, 131, 134
Teddington 12
Temple Guiting 18
Tennyson 73
Tetbury 100
Thames Head 141
Thames – River 13, 74, 112, 131, 132, 141,
    158
Thrupp 89
Tracy family 61
Turkdean 34, 35

Uley 105, 106, 108

Vanbrugh 34
Verey, David 121

Wade, Charles 59
Wemyss, Earl of 61
Weston-sub-Edge 12, 52
Whitmore family 28
Whittington 71
Whittington, Dick, Lord Mayor of London
    133
Willersey 12, 52, 53, 58
William the Conqueror 78
William III 40
Windrush – River 13, 18, 20, 22, 24, 25, 29,
    31, 34, 35, 41, 42, 45, 61, 144
Windrush 29, 30, 31, 34
Winstone 96
Wisdom, Simon 39
Withington 114, 117
Witney 45, 112
Woodchester 111
Wotton-under-Edge 13, 46, 102, 103
Wren, Sir Christopher 34
Wyck Rissington 31

Yanworth 117
Young, Charles Baring 155, 156

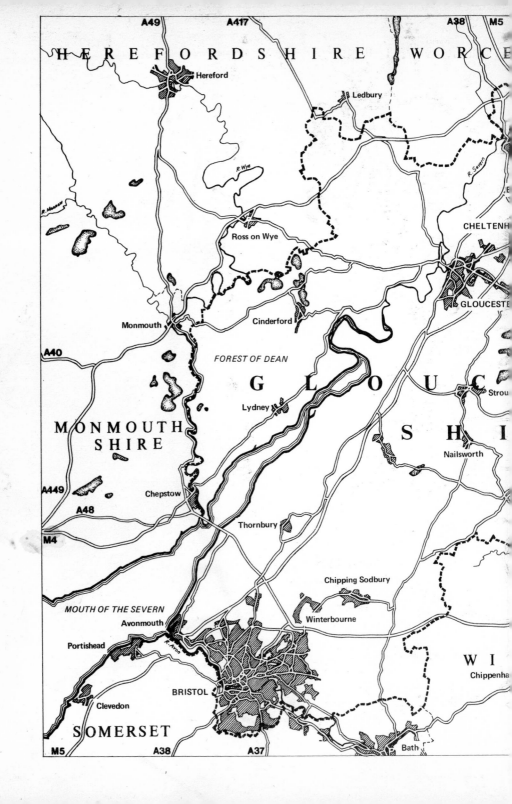